Plate I
Detail of inside front cover

BK 709.54   K89U
UNKNOWN INDIA; RITUAL ART IN TRIBE AND VILLAGE
                                        /KRAMRISCH,
1968   10.95   FV

3000 386911 30018
St. Louis Community College

WITHDRAWN

W9-DHM-637

709.54 K89u   EV
KRAMRISCH
  UNKNOWN INDIA; RITUAL ART
IN TRIBE AND VILLAGE
                              10.95

St. Louis Community
College

Library

5801 Wilson Avenue
St. Louis, Missouri 63110

Plate II
Village sanctuary of Aiyanar; Chettampatti
(Tiruchirapalli)

Plate III
Village shrine of Bhagavati Amman; Ganapathipalayam
(Kodamudi)

Plate v

Shrine of Muniapan (showing images of the Seven
Sisters); Vadugapalayam (Coimbatore)

Village shrine of Aiyanar; Nallur (Tiruchirapalli)

Plate VIII
Temple of Irulansami; Manalur (Madura)

Plate IX, catalogue number 1
Humped Bull
Mohenjo-Daro, West Pakistan
Terra-cotta; 2⅝″ x 2″ x 1¼″
Later part 3rd millennium B.C.
National Museum, New Delhi

Plate x, catalogue number 147
Elephant Rider (Ancestral Image)
Jagdalpur, Bastar, Madhya Pradesh
Brass; 4¾″ x 4¾″ x 1½″
17th century

Plate XI, catalogue number 27
Equestrian Figurine
Rajasthan
Brass; 5⅛″ x 3½″ x 1⁹⁄₁₆″
17th century

Plate XII, catalogue number 25
Equestrian Figurine
Rajasthan
Brass; 4¾" x 5" x 1"
16th-17th century

Plate XIII, catalogue number 26
Equestrian Figurine
Rajasthan
Brass; 4¾″ x 3¾″ x 1⅛″
17th century

Plate xɪv, catalogue number 34
Equestrian Figurine
Rajasthan
Brass; 4¾″ x 4⅛″ x 1¼″
18th century

Plate xv, catalogue number 228
Equestrian Figurine
Bihar
Brass; 4½″ x 4½″ x 2½″
18th century

Plate xvi, catalogue number 31
Equestrian Figurine
Rajasthan
Brass; 3⅜″ x 3⅛″ x 1⅜″
18th century

Plate XVII, catalogue number 233
Antelope
Bihar
Brass; 4½″ x 3¼″ x 2½″
18th century

Plate xviii, catalogue number 234
Antelope
Bihar
Brass; 6″ x 5″ x 3⅛″
18th century

Plate XIX, catalogue number 285
Navagunjara
Orissa
Brass; 8⅛″ x 7⅞″
ca. 19th century
Nalini and Haridas K. Swali

Plates xx and xxi, catalogue number 46
Dipa-Lakshmi
North Gujarat
Brass; 1′6⅛″ x 9″
18th century

Plate XXII, catalogue number 89

Demon
South India
Brass; 1'1½" x 5¼" x 5"
ca. 17th century
J. J. Klejman, New York

Plate xxiii, catalogue number 456
Standing Couple
Konyak Tribe, Nagaland
Wood; 11⅞" x 5½" x 4⅞"
20th century
National Museum, New Delhi

Plate XXIV, catalogue numbers 291, 292
Warrior and Female Figure
Kutiya Kond Tribe, Orissa – Andhra Pradesh border
Brass; both 7⅛″ x 2¾″ x 2″
19th century
Victoria and Albert Museum, London

Plate xxv, catalogue number 262
Fiddle
Santal Tribe, Bihar
Wood; 2'9¼" x 9⅞" x 6¾"
19th-20th century
National Museum, New Delhi

Plate xxv, catalogue number 152
Ceremonial "Doll"
Muria Tribe, Bastar, Madhya Pradesh
Wood; 1'4½" x 4¼"
20th century
National Museum, New Delhi

Plate xxvi, catalogue number 327
Carved Pilaster from a Processional Car of Jagannatha
Moisadal, West Bengal
Wood; 7' x 6" x 1'
Early 19th century
Victoria and Albert Museum, London

Plate xxvii, catalogue number 328
Carved Pilaster from a Processional Car of Jagannatha
Moisadal, West Bengal
Wood; 7′ x 6″ x 1′
Mid-19th century
Victoria and Albert Museum, London

Plate XXIX, catalogue number 182
Shadow Play Puppet: Sita
Andhra Pradesh
Leather, cut, painted and oiled; 4′ x 2′4″
First half 19th century
Crafts Museum, New Delhi

Plate xxx, catalogue number 153

Mask
Bhuiya Tribe, Bonai, Orissa – Madhya Pradesh border
Wood; 10⅞″ x 6¼″
20th century
National Museum, New Delhi

Plate XXXI, catalogue number 156
Mask
Bisonhorn Maria Tribe, Bastar, Madhya Pradesh
Wood, with hair affixed; 9¾″ x 6¼″
20th century
National Museum, New Delhi

Plate xxxii (detail), catalogue number 380
Krishna Lila Pat (Scroll Painting of the Life of Krishna)
Midnapur, West Bengal
Gouache on paper; 12'9½" x 1'9"
19th century

Plate XXXIII (detail), catalogue number 367B
Ramayana Pat
Hooghly, West Bengal
Gouache on paper; 1′5″ x 1′8″
Early 19th century

Plate xxxiv, catalogue number 390

Woman and Parrot
Kalighat
Brush drawing on paper; 1′5¼″ x 10¼″
ca. 1875

Plate xxxv (detail), catalogue number 189
Durga Killing the Buffalo Demon (Mahishasuramardini)
Panjab or Himachal Pradesh
Slate; 11″ x 5¾″ x ¾″
8th century

Plate xxxvi, catalogue number 205
Durga Killing the Buffalo Demon (Mahishasuramardini)
Kulu, Himachal Pradesh
Brass; 5″ x 4″
ca. 18th century
C. L. Bharany, New Delhi

Plate xxxvii, catalogue number 261
Veiled Bride, with Fish and Parrot
Darema, Darbhanga, North Bihar
Watercolours; 1'1" x 9"
ca. 1920-1930
Mildred and W. G. Archer Collection

Plate xxxviii (detail), catalogue number 439
Kantha
Faridpur, East Pakistan
Cotton embroidered cotton quilt; 2′5″ x 2′5½″
Second half 19th century

Plate xxxix (detail), catalogue number 416
Kantha
Khulna, East Pakistan
Cotton and silk embroidered cotton quilt; 7½″ x 2′
Late 19th to early 20th century

Plate XL, catalogue number 195
Canopy
Bahraich, Uttar Pradesh
Appliquéd cotton cloth; 15′3″ x 6′1″
Early 20th century
Mildred and W. G. Archer Collection

Plate xLi (detail), catalogue number 442
Kantha
Faridpur, East Pakistan
Cotton embroidered cotton quilt; 4'11" x 3'3"
19th century

Plate XLII, catalogue number 414
Kantha
Khulna, East Pakistan
Cotton embroidery on white quilt; 2′8¾″ x 2′7″
Early 19th century

Plate XLIII (detail), catalogue number 443
Kantha
Faridpur, East Pakistan
Cotton embroidered cotton quilt; 2′5¾″ x 2′2″
Late 19th to early 20th century

Plate XLIV (detail), catalogue number 256
Kamalban
Darema, Darbhanga, North Bihar
Coloured ink on paper; 1'1" x 1'4"
ca. 1920-1940
Mildred and W. G. Archer Collection

Plate XLV (detail), catalogue number 443
Kantha
Faridpur, East Pakistan
Cotton embroidered cotton quilt; 2'5¾" x 2'2"
Late 19th to early 20th century

Plate XLVI, catalogue number 433
Kantha
Faridpur, East Pakistan
Cotton embroidered cotton quilt; 2′5½″ x 2′6¼″
Second half 19th century

Plate xlvii (detail), catalogue number 435
Kantha
Faridpur, East Pakistan
Cotton embroidered cotton quilt; 5′6½″ x 3′10¼″
Late 19th century

Asha Danda
Sundarban, West Bengal
Brass; 8″ x 5¼″
20th century

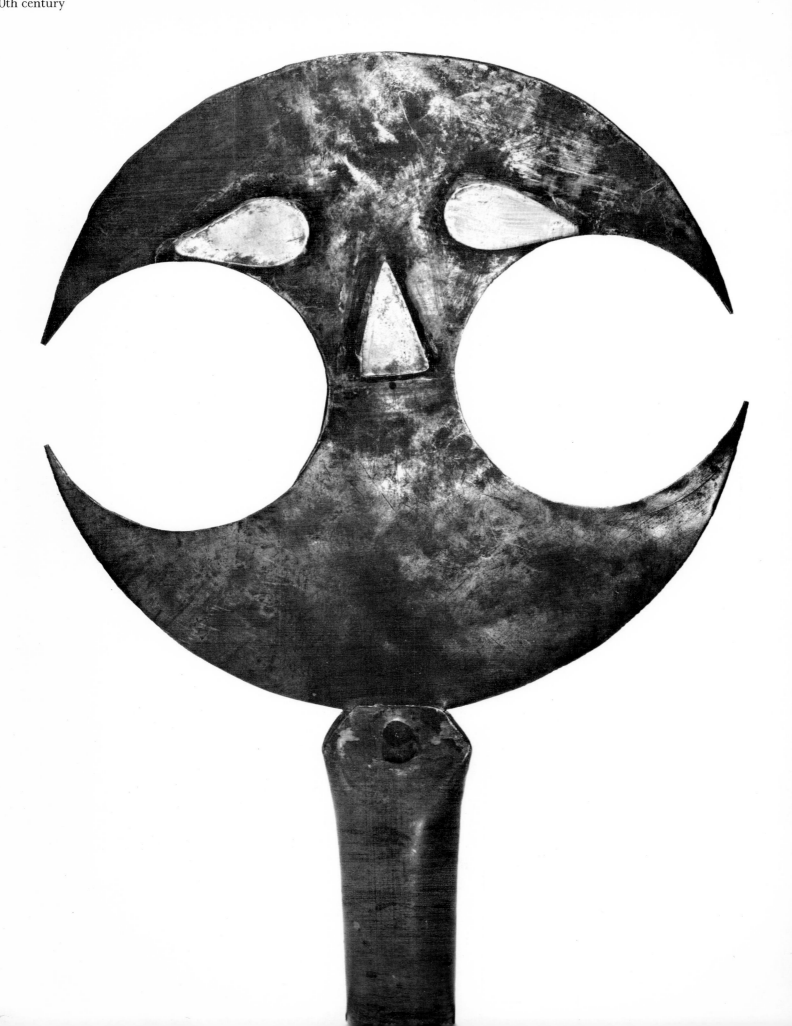

Unknown India:
Ritual Art in Tribe and Village

by Stella Kramrisch

The Setting

Over the landscape of Indian art tower the great stone temples, the profusion of
their sculptures tempered by the elegance of their form. Into the substance itself
of the earth, earlier centuries had cut their sanctuaries, had transmuted the living
rock into gigantic visions of deity, vibrant in depth. The artists, as a rule, came from
the lower strata of the social fabric of India. Many of them were of peasant stock. The
organization of their guilds was built upon the close contact between their rural
homes and their calling, which took them away from their homes and in which they
carried out the visions and speculations of the spiritual élite. This close cooperation
having ended, Indian art lost its guidance and patronage. The need was felt no
longer to build or excavate a temple that would endure and secure for the patron a
place in heaven while still on earth. The villages, however, continued with very little
change in their own fabric or in their needs.

The great temples today rise as monuments of the past over a landscape that stayed
productive though impoverished in its means, that stayed alive from generation to
generation with the course of the years and the seasons, with the waxing and waning
of the moon, with sunrise and sunset. All these moments and transitions have their
response in innumerable rites and in countless shapes, many of which are not meant
to last—moulded in clay or made of wood or cotton—for they will be made again and
again with the rites of spring or autumn, with the daily rites of evocation. They are
part of the sacraments of living, invoking an invisible superhuman presence whose
reality is contacted and communicated by those shapes. But for them it would
remain beyond reach and control.

The Indian rural economy of art provides for sculptures to be made as offerings to
the deity and to be left untended at the place where they were given, under a tree,
near pond or river or in a grove (plates: cover, inside front cover, I-III, VI-VIII). They
accumulate, they decompose, and others take their place. It is not the form which
remains and endures, but the performance which makes the form and gives it style,
changing with the years as do the leaves on the trees and eventually the trees
themselves, yet recognisable in its local varieties as part of the scene where the
sculptures stand. Each scene had its "genius loci," called *yaksha*. Such genii controlled
the sacred geography of India in ancient times when they were called by this name.
This was even before the millennium when the stone temples were built as works of
monumental sculpture, showing forth on their walls the figure of man transmuted into
the likeness of gods (ca. 500 to 1500 A.D.). Ancient Indian texts on architecture such
as the Samaranganasutradhara of the eleventh century designate the majority of the
temples as *nagara*. This means "belonging to a town." It was there in the towns,
preeminently, that a royal patron would endow a temple, greater in its height and
splendour and more durable in its material than any palace. It was there that the
Brahmans, the priests, laid down the guiding lines and the Kshatriyas, the nobility,
set the standards of discriminating taste.

Today, as in former times, there are many large towns in India, but few large temples
have been built during the last centuries, under Muslim and British rule. The Great
Tradition of architectural sculpture died a slow death. Today, as in former times, the
people of India—now about five hundred millions—are mainly, that is, eighty-two
percent, rural. Moreover, eighty percent of the rural population worship other gods

than Vishnu and Shiva who are worshipped by Brahmans in the large temples.

Only about thirty millions are counted today as tribal. Practically half of the tribal population of Middle and South India do not declare themselves as Hindu.[1] If outside the pale of Hindu influences, and left to themselves, they neither built temples nor did they make images of their gods. Their religion expresses itself directly in rites in which works of art are the indispensable and focal means of communication with the supernatural, with man's experience of the Real. The Real is sensed in the waking experience. It may be adumbrated in dreams. It is known in trance. Trance, dream and waking experiences are actual though they vary in kind and degree and lie in different but interconnected planes. Tribal art gives them form.

Amongst the tribal people of India, the Gond, Santal, and Bhil are the most numerous groups. They are called aboriginal inasmuch as they were in India before the Aryans arrived in the middle of the second millennium B.C. However, before that time a great urban civilisation, with its capital cities in the Panjab and Sind, had extended over a large part of the peninsula (third to second millennium B.C.). The relation of the ancestors of the present tribal people to that great urban civilisation of Mohenjo-Daro and Harappa is not known.

Tribal art throughout India for the last two thousand years at least must be assumed to have coexisted with traditions commanding greater means and more complex organization. The Buddhist stone railings of the Stupa of Bharhut and the Stupa of the Saints, in Sanchi, both collective monuments of sculpture of the second to first century B.C., show the work of many different hands. These stone railings with their carvings are each a symposium of styles, some of which bear affinity to tribal carvings such as those of the Gond who to this day live not far from the sites of these ancient monuments. Buddhism was open to members of any group. The sculptors, however, were not necessarily Buddhists, they came from the lower Hindu strata of ancient Indian or tribal stock. Progressing Hinduization, while dissolving much of the self-supporting and self-sufficient tribal communities, absorbed as much as it destroyed of tribal traditions while these tribes, where they survived as solid groups, assimilated much from their suppressors who also were their neighbours. But Hinduism from the start is an alloy of the Brahmanic tradition and the many other and older Indian traditions. Due to this long process of osmosis, tribal art in India, on the whole, lacks the stylistic certitudes and perfectedness of the tribal art of Africa, Oceania, and of the American Indian. The art of the Naga, who live on the northeastern frontier of India, although relatively pure, is slighter; the art of tribal Mid-India cruder, and that of the Bhil more heterogeneous than Congo or Melanesian creations.

Of all the tribal people of India, the small group of the Toda, who live in the Nilgiris, the Blue Hills of South India, have left what may be considered the most ancient relics (about first century A.D.). Terra-cotta figurines, excavated there, are, it would seem, the work of their ancestors[2] (nos. 15-20). Some of these figurines have tribal forms, others do not essentially differ in some respects from some of the terra-cottas found in Mohenjo-Daro (nos. 1, 2; plate IX), while in certain respects some of the Mohenjo-Daro figurines can be compared with the work by village potters and women made to this day in Bengal (no. 22).

Today, the tribal people live in the less accessible parts of the country, not on the open plains, not along the great rivers. Whether they are of the Dravidian or Munda language family, the coherence of each tribe depends upon common rites, on the way the sacraments of life are celebrated and those of death. These make the fundamental identity of tribe and clan. Contacts with the surrounding rural Hindu population act both ways. Traditions are exchanged and prejudices are born. To some of the low-caste Hindus on the fringes of tribal society are delegated, by the tribal people, tasks to which the Hindus themselves do not assign high rank. The age-old profession of the potter is one of them.

Panini, the great grammarian in the fourth century B.C., distinguished between village craftsmen *(grama-shilpin)* and royal craftsmen *(raja-shilpin)* who worked for a feudal lord. This distinction, however, is not equivalent to one between folk art and court art though it assigns a different status to the practitioners of certain crafts, the potters being classified among the village craftsmen, their craft being practiced in the village itself. Just as the tribal people, who lived by hunting, food-gathering and shifting cultivation—some only practicing settled agriculture—are looked down upon by their neighbours, the Hindu peasants, with their settled agriculture and full-time specialized occupations, so too the tribal people in psychological revenge consider the lower of the peasant crafts, like that of the potter, below their own dignity. They make the non-tribal, low-caste Hindu potters work for them,[3] according to their own instructions. Their snobbery, however, has no effect on the work of the potter. Although he is outside the tribe, bonds of propinquity, and as likely as not of consanguinity, are stronger than prejudice. The object made by the potter, who shapes not only pots but also clay figures, exactly suits his tribal patron and the use for which he requires it. This use again does not essentially differ from the one a villager would have for the potter's work, for instance, for a clay horse.

Similarly, tribal people at present speak languages which are not their own but those of their neighbours. One and the same tribe, the Bhil, whose habitat ranges over a wide area, speak the languages of their nearest neighbour, be it Rajasthani, Gujarati or Marathi, although they also have their own language, Bhili, an Aryan tongue. The original tribal language however is forgotten, the words which accompany the rites of the Bhil are really not their own. And what about the works of art through which the Bhil—and their neighbours—perform their rites? Their styles differ from region to region (nos. 25-34, 143, 159; plates XI-XIV, XVI) as much as the languages through which the Bhil express their unmistakable identity.

The unknown art of India is the art created in village and tribe on social levels below and away from the towering temples. The tribal art of the Naga, on the northeastern frontier of India, and that of tribes in Mid-India remain relatively intact to this day. Apart from these traditions, rural India is a rich ground for cross-fertilisation, producing deceptive simplicities of styles in tribe and village. The tribal style of the Bhil, which encompasses a wide area, is shown in the exhibition by the figurine of the Spirit Rider. The village art of South India is represented in the exhibition by the sacred grove with its many and large clay figures, mainly of horses (plates: cover, VIII). When the horse was brought to India from its home in Inner Asia is not known. Long before the Aryans in the middle of the second millennium B.C. had entered India from the north on horseback, the tame horse was represented in Harappan terra-cotta figurines, unearthed in Lothal and Rangpur.[4] Horse riding later on was a privilege of the aristocracy, the Rajputs, the "sons of kings."

The essentially Indian tribal art form of the wide-ranging figurine of the Bhil Spirit Rider and the essentially Indian village art of the locally circumscribed cult of Aiyanar in which the figure of the horse is exalted show, on the one hand, a tribal identity at the base of a variety of styles and, on the other hand, an autochthonous and localized style brought about by the confluence of many traditions. If these two aspects of a particularly Indian artistic relevance are here singled out in introducing the unknown art of India, a third artistic type, characteristic in its all-Indian application and ramifications, must also be mentioned: the magic diagram, drawn on the floor, a form of art practiced by women only, or by non-Brahman priests on behalf of women.

The Spirit Rider

The archetype of all the figurines of horsemen which give reality to the Nukto rite of the Bhil has vanished from the scene. Its meaning and function, however, come to life whenever the rite is performed, and the mystery of death-in-life is once more confirmed through the figurine of the rider on his horse. It plays the leading role in this essential tribal rite of the Bhil, although the Bhil neither raise nor use horses. The equestrian figure in art and legend is generally associated with the feudal Hindu Rajputs, the northern neighbours of the Bhil.

The equestrian figure is one of the themes of art by which the tribal world and that of the feudal aristocracy are linked here on earth. Over and above this, its image is a magic link between heaven and earth. This is its purpose. In this respect, the function of the equestrian figurine is not different from that of the great temples which were erected in the cities. There, the ascent to heaven was built up, stone by stone, each stone carved with an image appropriate to its position in the entire edifice, piled high so that step by step the architectural ritual of the ascent became the monument, the temple. The architectural ritual is put into words in the ancient texts of that science. The oral tradition of the tribal Bhil to this day verifies step by step the journey of the soul which has the Spirit Rider for its acting support.

The liberating function of art is shared by the tribal non-Hindu, the Hindu peasant and the Hindu élite in one tribal-village-urban continuum, where the currents of art from tribe and village to the élite, from the élite to tribe and village, flow both ways.

The tribe of the Bhil, the "sons of the forest" (vanaputra), lives in Western India, from the Aravalli Mountains in Rajasthan to the Vindhya range. It is in and near this region that in the course of the last two thousand years the Buddhist cave temples and monasteries of Ajanta were cut out of the rocks, the Jains built the marble temples at Mount Abu, and many Hindu shrines have borne witness to the experience of the numinous. The Bhil were hunters, fishermen and food-gatherers— they have learned animal husbandry from their neighbours, the Gujar—and they are agriculturists. Although centered in Rajasthan (Mewar), Gujarat, and Khandesh, they also live in loosely connected groups in the mountains and the less readily accessible parts of Sind (in Pakistan), Kutch, and Rajasthan in the northwest and in the state of Andhra in the southeast. A small group of them is found as far to the northeast as Bengal.[5] Said to be of pre-Aryan origin, they are classified as proto-Australoid or as Veddid.[6] Their original language is lost; they form a psychological complex without linguistic, physiognomic, economic or cultural unity.[7] Their spirituality is their own and holds them together.

Formerly they ruled over their own country. This was prior to the arrival of the Rajputs. The Rajputs, the "sons of kings," invaded the country, subsequently Rajasthan, in about the sixth century A.D. They became Kshatriyas, the nobility par excellence of India. Some of these Rajput princes including the most exalted of them, the Rana of Mewar, at the inception of their rule, had their forehead marked with the blood of a Bhil. It was drawn from his thumb or big toe.[8] This was an acknowledgement of the precedence of the Bhil as rulers of the country.

The Rajputs are horse owners and riders. The Bhil use the image of the horseman; it is that of a Spirit Rider (no. 159), the Gothriz Purvez, the Ancestor of the clan. On it is focused the solidarity of the clan; it redeems the dead and liberates the living from the fear of death and the despair of loneliness. Moreover, the Bhil commemorate their fallen heroes, killed in a fight or cattle-raid, by setting up stone memorial slabs carved in low relief with an equestrian figure; whereas memorial stones set up for their dead by others, the Rajputs in particular, frequently have a standing figure in front view (nos. 35, 36).[9] The Bhil confer on their ancestors the nobility of the horseman, the chevalier whereas the Rajputs do not particularly stress the equestrian form of their dead. From the hymns of the Rig Veda (second half of second millennium B.C.) the group of horse and rider is vested with sacredness. Indra, the Creator God, rode the horse for the first time.[10] Later tradition knows the Sun God as rider[11] and the horse itself as fire in all its aspects, on earth and in heaven, the sun on high and the spark of life.[12]

The Bhil ritual for the dead is celebrated in front of the entrance of the house of the deceased.[13] From above its lintel a twelve-runged bamboo ladder is suspended and subsequently also a long string with an arrow—the Bhil were primarily hunters—attached to it. This man-made setting and its paraphernalia contrast with the sacred grove, the central sanctuary of every Bhil settlement. There, an unhewn stone or stones are the symbols of deity. In the cult of the dead, however, man is the symbol. The anthropomorphic image and representation, which are here those of the horseman, are linked with the cult of the dead. Another object required for the great Nukto rite, the rite of the dead, is the figurine of a cow. These figurines are made of the copper anklets of the widow of the deceased. The material itself of the figurines has magical virtue; it takes part in the ritual and undergoes a spiritual alchemy.

The Gothriz Purvez is placed on an altar, the cow on a metal tray. The long string leads to the altar of the Gothriz Purvez and thence to the cow. Now the scene is set. The main actors are the Rawal, the master of ceremonies, the Barwo, the magician, and the Waha, the priest. The Waha, who acts as a Brahman or priest, is a male child from the clan of the dead person.

The preparation for the Nukto rite begins when the Rawal sings to the dying man at the first *ghanto,* corresponding to the first rung of the ladder: "Alone go, brother, to Bhagavan (the Supreme God) through the seven depths." And at the third *ghanto,* the Rawal speaks over the dead body: "Come, quite alone." And at the fifth *ghanto,* it is the spirit *(jiva)* who speaks: "I am alone, brother, I am alone." The rungs of the bamboo ladder which the Rawal had hung from the doorframe, represent the twelve stations of the mountain with their obstacles which the *jiva,* the spirit, has to climb before it is purified and reaches Bhagavan.

The Bhil distinguish between the body, the psychic elements or the ghost *(bhuta)* and shadow, and the spirit *(jiva)* of man. They separate at death. The body is cremated; a heap of stones is piled up under a tree. There the *bhuta* is appeased in the first three days of the rites, after the death of the body. On the fourth day, the Nukto rites of three days begin. It is then that the Rawal ties the string on the wooden crossbar above the entrance. When the *jiva* has attained the seventh rung the stones are scattered; there is now no resting place on earth for any part of the man who died. The spirit rises from one rung of tests and judgement to the next, overcoming the obstacles of each rung. The spirit is purified during the ascent. In the night when the spirit has passed the tenth and eleventh rungs and has been judged in the twelve courts, it goes to Bhagavan. The Rawal has sprinkled the cow with milk to make the spirit pure and white. When the spirit has completed its ascent, during the first Nukto rite, on the fourth day after death, the twelve rungs of the ladder are destroyed, the spirit descends along the string into the arrow, the Rawal having poured water thrice over the cow. By these rites, the spirit is further purified. The spirit now enters the equestrian figurine and the cow and overcomes the Barwo, who, having undergone in the meanwhile the necessary preparations, is in trance. The spirit makes the Barwo select the Waha, a young boy from the clan of the dead, who is now consecrated. The Waha is the Gothriz Purvez; he is possessed by the spirit and is given the same name as the rider figurine on the horse who is the Gothriz Purvez, the Ancestor of the clan, the liberated spirit of the man who had died. The Waha, trembling in his trance, holds the tablet with the figurine of the cow, while the Rawal sings for the *khatariz* (Kshatriya), the hero, the spirit.

When the figurine of the cow, held by the trembling Waha, has itself ceased to tremble, it is taken in procession to the tree where the stones were collected and then were scattered. The figurine of the cow is buried.

The Rawal tears the string on which the spirit has descended. The Waha is no longer possessed by the spirit. The purified spirit (*jiva*) has been accepted in the clan of the ancestors. It dwells with Bhagavan, in the beyond. The Nukto rite has been completed. A meal and mask-dance follow.

Without the Nukto rite, the spirit could not have been purified, could not have ascended to Bhagavan and found its place. It would have remained alone, erring between here and there, troubling the heart and mind of the clansmen. The effigy of the spirit (*jiva*), the Gothriz Purvez, the equestrian metal statuette, remains with them. It is not buried as is the figurine of the cow.

The double embodiment of the purified spirit as Ancestor of the clan, in the living body of the entranced youth of the clan, the Waha, and in the equestrian metal statuette proves both to be its temporary abodes. For this, the Waha was made fit by his trance, and the equestrian statuette by its form. The figurine of the cow, too, is temporarily the place where the spirit dwells. But when this figurine ceases to tremble, the spirit has left it, and the little metal cow is buried, having served its purpose. Very few metal figurines of cows exist. The number of equestrian metal figurines is large. They vary considerably in shape, each variation having a formal consistency of its own. They are set up frequently also in household shrines of Rajputs and other Hindus.

Without the figurine of the Gothriz Purvez, the spirit of the dead could not be purified and could not reach Bhagavan, the Supreme God. The figurine, the work of art, is an essential means towards the clan's attainment of a feeling of spiritual worth and earthly security, a feeling of peace and solidarity. The liberated spirit, the *khatariz,* the hero, comes to dwell in the Nukto rite amidst the clan, in the living, young body of the Waha and in the equestrian statuette.

The Waha discharged the function of a Brahman. For this purpose, he was invested, like a Brahman, with a sacred thread. It is not only in this instance that the Bhil raise a child to the status of a Brahman or recognise in a child a special power.[14] It is the power of the assumed innocence of the child.[15]

The equestrian metal figurines, essential part of rites and trance, were however not made during a trance experience. Invariably cast by the lost wax process, they fall into different stylistic groups. In one particularly spirited variety, a special technique of casting contributed to the tense alertness of its form. But to whatever thought and style-type of figurines horse and rider may belong, they seem to have come from a world of enchantment where innocence and trusting pride went into their conception. Their form lacks not only the tension and determination of similar ancient Iranian metal figurines,[16] but also the cursive, fluid generalization of comparable animal figurines made of clay by Tallensi children of the African Gold Coast.[17] Essentially metallic in character, the pristine, though not primitive, figurines assignable to the Bhil ambience, whether made by Bhil or by Hindu metalsmiths, show rider and horse advancing, as it were, though the legs of the horse are always firmly planted on the ground (nos. 25-34, 143, 159; plates XI-XIV, XVI). With one hand the rider holds the reins, as a rule, in the other a staff or weapon. His head is raised, the back is straight. With the four feet of the horse on the ground, the seemingly advancing movement of the group is effected by the position and spacing of the legs of the horse and also by the position and spacing of the neck and head of the horse and the body of the rider, the latter frequently inclining backward. Self-contained and static, the entire group appears as if drawn forward by an invisible pull. Though three-dimensional, it is complete in its silhouette. Seen from various angles, rider and horse show themselves in ever new responses of their masses and the connecting voids, left intact by the unobtrusiveness of the rider's legs. Like short, flattened ribbons, the rider's legs adhere to the body of the horse and do not exceed the length of the saddle, as a rule. It is the reins, arms, and weapon which enhance the airiness and onward pull of the group. Whether of

Don Quixotian elegance as in Rajasthan (nos. 25-30; plates xi-xiii), or full-bodied as also in Rajasthan (nos. 31-33; plate xvi), Malwa (West Madhya Pradesh) and in Khandesh (Maharashtra), with the rider's face planar and presenting its features as ridges (nos. 29-30) according to the standards of tribal art; or with a three-dimensional face, abstractly modelled and pinched into the peak of the nose (no. 27; plate xi); or more naturalistically organized and with the horse's legs flexed and articulated (no. 34; plate xiv)—or simply as sturdy cylinders—each group has a serenely harmonious balance of its own for the liberated spirit, the Ancestor of the clan to dwell in. As this spirit in the Nukto rite takes possession of the Waha, a child, so its image in turn embodies the immortal spirit of childhood as Ancestor of the clan.

Cast by the lost wax process, these figurines are distinct from the nervy zest of the thin-legged horses and frisky riders cast hollow in a special "wire" technique[18] (nos. 228-231; plate xv). It is practiced by the quasi-Hinduized metalworkers of the Kainkuya Mal caste, also called Dhokra, a migratory, and partly settled caste of metalsmiths who came from Bihar to Bengal; by the Malar who are said to have come to Bihar from Madhya Pradesh and by the Kaser in Bastar, Madhya Pradesh. By their technique of hollow bronze casting, where a ribbed surface results (often it is subsequently smoothed) from placing wax "wires," one-tenth of an inch thick, one against the other, and over them more wax wires, forming an ornamental relief pattern, an eery elegance is obtained in the figurines from Bihar of which not only the horse but also the deer or antelope are chosen embodiments. Like the other small metal images here described, the antelopes too were kept on house altars (nos. 233-241; plates xvii, xviii). Warding off evil spirits, they are spirit guardians of manifold meaning. Brahmanic tradition tells of Prajapati, the Lord of Progeny, the creator "per generationem," who committed incest with his daughter, an antelope.[19] Vivasvant, the sun, in the shape of a horse, mated with Samjna, a mare. She was the daughter of Vishvakarman, the Maker of the Universe, the creator "per artem."[20] Impetuous and fleet, horse and antelope or deer are symbols of creativeness, full of secret redeeming and protective power.[21] As such, they live in the art of the castes of the metalworkers in Eastern India.

Related to their style and technique of work is that of the Kaser, or Ghasia, of Madhya Pradesh (nos. 148, 149). It lacks the gracile phantasy of their work, and its wire texture is more involved and inventive. The figurines are often ponderous,[22] at other times they are phantasmagorias of delicate spikes (no. 147; plate x).

The figurine of the horseman as a Spirit Rider is not always the focal point of a trance experience. As an image of the spirit freed from the human condition, it represents a state of perfection and fulfillment in which immortal heroes dwell. Representing a state of fulfillment, it is credited with the power of granting fulfillment—of wishes and desires (nos. 51-56). When made of clay it is an offering — to a god or hero like Kasumar Damor, a great magician, helper of the Barwo and tutelary spirit of the people. At his mountain sanctuary such images, many on wheels, are deposited, and also clay horses, as part of vows and as votive gifts when the need is felt for having a child, regaining health, winning a court case or for success as a robber.[23] Made of clay, the image is reduced to its minimal form and is part of the vast, timeless world of clay figurines into which history and legend may delve and give specific actuality and meaning to a perennial theme[24] (nos. 1, 5-7, 10, 356; plate ix). Images of seventy-two horsemen are installed on a platform somewhere in Kutch.[25] They commemorate, legend tells, and keep as potent helpers, those white-skinned foreigners said to have come in the thirteenth century from Anatolia and Syria and to have killed the tyrant Punvaro. He had cut off the hands of the architect who had built the city of Patan so that he might not construct anything like it again. The seventy-two horsemen took the fort and killed the chief.[26] Harking back to other, untold memories from Inner Asian horse-herding cultures, these apocalyptic horsemen transmute the fear generated by Muslim invasions into India into a liberating legend in which the evil power does not come from outside but is local, embodied in the tyrant Punvaro. His heinous crime and its punishment are in the Great Indian Tradition. Capital punishment awaits the person who incapacitates a practicing artist[27] and prevents creativeness from functioning. The veneration of the creative act and the annihilation of the obstructor are mythologized in the battle of the Creator God, Indra—who was the first to ride a horse—with the serpent dragon Vritra, who had prevented the creative waters from flowing. The heroic horseman—far more than the sacred cow—had taken hold of the imagination of the Indian sculptor in tribe and village.

Autochthony

In South India, in almost every Tamil village there is a shrine of Aiyanar.[28] Often a large, rough stone without any carving is set up under a tree. It stands for the presence of Aiyanar. Such a stone setting belongs to tribal tradition. But Aiyanar is a Brahman deity and his worshippers are Dravidian villagers. Generally his sanctuary is on the banks of a pond. Its waters fertilize the fields which he protects. In some of his sanctuaries, Aiyanar is represented in human shape, a kingly figure riding a horse or an elephant. Horses are offered to him, large terra-cotta horses, so that he does not lack a mount during the watches of the night when he rides around the village and looks after its safety. He rides with his retinue of heroes—and demons. Two horses at least must be offered to Aiyanar each year. The second is for Karuppan, the Dark God, the demon who accompanies him. Over the years, the horses accumulate in the sacred groves. Up to five hundred such large clay horses (up to ten feet or more) may be ready in one sanctuary for the nocturnal rides (plate vi/vii). New horses are set up, while the old and broken ones are left to decay and return to the earth of which they were made. Under the image of Aiyanar a stone linga, the phallic symbol of Shiva's creativeness, is buried. The seed of Shiva, from which Aiyanar was born, it is said, fell near the banks of the waters.

The numinous lives integrally in Aiyanar's sanctuaries, in the waters near by and in the soil, in the trees which enshrine the multitude of clay horses in their upright splendour and in their decay where, fallen to the ground, they are left to return to the earth whose mystery emanates from the total setting and pervades the heterogeneous but utterly consistent legend of Aiyanar (plate vi/vii). These open-air South Indian village sanctuaries are replete with a living art and the living knowledge of the underlying myth whose components and ritual range from Brahmanic to tribal tradition. The salient points of the myth are here put down so that the majesty of form of these clay horses may be comprehended in its proper perspective.

Aiyanar, the Lord, is the son of the two great Hindu gods—Shiva, the ascetic Creator-Destroyer; and Vishnu, the Preserver. In order to arouse Shiva, Vishnu assumed the shape of a wonderfully beautiful girl called Mohini, or Delusion. She excited Shiva, and he let his seed fall near the waters. From it, Aiyanar, the son of Shiva and Vishnu (Hariharaputra) was born. A king, while hunting, found the beautiful babe lying on the ground, crying but his face radiant with a thousand suns.

The main sanctuary of Aiyanar, the Lord, is in the thickly wooded Shabari hills in Kerala near the western coast of South India. There the Lord protects man from evil spirits and endows him with knowledge which leads to salvation. But in the sanctuary of Erumeli in Kerala, Aiyanar is worshipped in the form of a hunter.[29] His devotees dance wildly when they worship the Lord of this world of delusion, might and fear.

Neither the wisdom aspect nor the orgiastic one are overtly part of the divinity of Aiyanar in the eastern, Tamil part of South India (he is not known north of the Godavari River), but the mystery of his birth from the two great Hindu gods passed on to the potency of the waters and the earth of any particular locality where Aiyanar is worshipped. While he is the same everywhere, each time it is a different Aiyanar who is worshipped[30] (no. 123; plates: inside front cover, ii, vi/vii).

The Lord, Aiyanar, the guardian of the land, has his generals and lieutenants. They are heroes *(vira)*, that is they are the souls of those who died in battle. They are joined by the host of demons (no. 100), foremost Karuppan (no. 84), the Dark God, who is all that Aiyanar is not. He is the adversary to whom blood sacrifices are due. Aiyanar is worshipped with flowers and fruits. The dark power within Aiyanar, the Hunter, has been hypostatized into Karuppan, his alter ego, the demon as protector. Together, they are worshipped by the officiating priest who also is the maker of their images. He is the village potter, a Kusavan by caste, son of a Brahman father and a low-cast *(shudra)* mother. During worship he becomes possessed by Karuppan, the Dark God, the alter ego of Aiyanar. Other names of Aiyanar are also Bhutanatha, Lord of Demons, and Dharma Shasta, "in front of whom all laws *(dharma)* of society to which a person belongs must be abandoned" so that his presence is realized.

The terra-cotta steeds are offered to Aiyanar by the village collectively or by individual devotees. Larger than real, the horses raise their fiercely noble heads, ready to carry god or demon. The potter-priest gives them basic shapes which he knows how to modify in keeping with the ardent naturalism of South Indian sculpture. He has seen the rearing stone horses supporting the roofs of the large halls of stone temples of the Vijayanagar style of the sixteenth century.

Himself potter and priest, he moulds the clay horses, impressing the clay with tensions experienced in shamanistic possession. The clay itself is taken from a ground of sacred fertility. It holds the linga of Shiva and the seed from which Aiyanar has sprung. Aiyanar, the Lord, scion of the two great Hindu gods, King of Demons, synthesis of deity experienced on the many levels of India's religious structure, depends on the clay horses offered to him for his rides. Their power is vested in the soil from which they are made. It does not extend beyond the Tamil village and its autochthonous art.

Other South Indian open-air sanctuaries are consecrated to the Goddess (plates: cover, III, IV). In her sevenfold aspect, she is worshipped as the Seven Virgins. The sacred grove may be a square enclosure. The image of the Seven Heavenly Virgins are moulded as one mass barely accentuated in its sevenfold undulating identity. The Seven Sisters form a sacred unit (cf. plate v) and are the tutelary deities of ponds. They go in procession with horses and torches. Whoever sees them, dies.[31] These Seven Virgins with their will-of-the-wisp, wide-open, painted eyes hold amongst themselves the message of death—and the power over birth. They guard against evil. They, too, are offered horses.

The ancient Aryans sacrificed a horse to Varuna, the god of the fertilizing waters. In hymnic intoxication, they knew the horse as Varuna (Rig Veda I. 163. 4). They knew it for the horse had risen from the waters, from the primal fount of life (Rig Veda I. 163. 1). To the South Indian Dravidian peasant of today, this hymnic realization of the fiery animal, the horse, of the fiery spark of life that is in the waters, of the fire that at daybreak seems to arise from the waters as glowing sun (cf. also no. 421) and sinks into their darkness and dies, has become uncannily one with the power of Aiyanar and also with the eery, fatal Seven Virgins. They have sprung from the soil, from swamp and pond, these autochthonous goddesses. They are ancient and local and have taken to them the steed that India had known long before the Aryans had come with their horses to India from the north. The Kusavan, the potter-priest, Aryan-Brahman and aboriginal by his blood, is competent to conceive and make the images of the Seven Sisters in the sanctuary of Muniapan and give it the sacred shape of the square, the symbol of cosmic order (plate v). The clear-cut symmetry of this sanctuary combines a mastery over many levels of experience compressed in its extent. In the Seven Virgins and also in many female votive images offered in the sacred groves, primary shapes are suffused with a visionary power (plate v). The content of tribal and rural art springs from primary concerns. They are those of life, death and transcendence in man and of life and death in the cosmos of which he is part.

The form of the work of tribal and rural art of India is, in each of the two hitherto discussed instances, a product of heterogeneous provenance and actuality of purpose. Elsewhere in India, recent tribal art lacks the integrated strength of tribal art in Africa and is generally only an offshoot of what it could have been. Even where its character has not been diluted, its vigour has been sapped. But the loss of character of tribal art is the gain of the rural art of India. By a process of osmosis, the essence of tribal art flowed into rural art. There it has been shown that it is the priest who made the clay horses and other images. While performing the rites, he becomes possessed by Karuppan, the Dark God. Possession and trance of the priest as performer follow upon his work as maker or former of the sculptures which carry or contain the spirit that will possess him.

Amongst the tribal people of the Bhil, the work of art—an equestrian figurine—was an integral and focal point of a rite. Without it, the rite has no validity. The figurine is a locus of identification with the supernatural. Without it, this identification could not be established. It requires, however, the participation of a priest in trance to become effective. Here, artist and priest, though not combined in one person, are united as form and performer.

The Spirit Riders of the Bhil, Aiyanar with his equestrian retinue of heroes and demons, have each their own locale, myths and rites. The form of the sculptures is their visual equivalent and residue. Less rich in myth and rites are the traditions of the Spirit Riders who guard the villages all over India and whose equestrian images and votive horses are made by the village potters in basic, primary shapes[32] (no. 190).[33] They all ride without stirrups, on saddled or unsaddled horses.[33] Where no rider is figured plastically, the living human medium in his frenzy may symbolically mount a clay horse by putting his toes on it.[34]

The horse is one of the main themes in the tribal and rural art of India. It rode deep into the interior of the country, carrying the liberated spirit and its own nobility, power and fertility. It brings wish fulfillment to the poor and the suppressed; it is the hobbyhorse ridden by the followers of Shiva in Bengal at the Gambhira Festival in the Night of Shiva (Shivaratri), a wooden or bamboo stick with coloured paper and string (no. 363); or it is a dancing horse which takes part in the dance in this festival[35] and also in others, in other seasons of the year, in other parts of the country as in Tanjore, in the south.

The symbol "horse" carries the hopes of everyman in India. It has vivified the creative imagination of village potters and tribal craftsmen and is an outpost of their innumerable styles. Known in India from the remotest past, once more, carrying its Aryan rider, it had entered India from on high, from the north, across the mountains and the social and ethnical strata of the country.

Horses are offered to any village god, male or female.[36] Deposits of clay horses abound not only in the sacred groves of South India or the western hills where Kasumar Dhamor protects his people, but also near the village shrines of Bengal, on the graves of Hindu Tantrik and of Muslim saints. By an irony of creative justice, the village potter makes clay horses in their basic timeless shapes, not only for the aboriginal and lowly (the members of the "scheduled castes") but also at the order of the high castes, the Brahmans and Kshatriyas. These spirit horses and riders are massed for worship in a Brahmasthana.[37] The name means "Place of Brahma" and is the traditional name, in ancient architectural treatises,[38] for the site of the innermost sanctuary of a stone temple of the Great Tradition. The Spirit Rider here represents "the soul of a benevolent, unmarried Brahmin."[39]

The figure of the horse in the art of tribal and rural India retained its basic shape, particularly in the small terra-cotta images (nos. 6, 7, 10), alongside with a form which had become more complex by assimilating to its own simplicity the naturalism which was part of the Great Tradition of Indian sculpture, as in the Tamil village horses (plates: cover, inside front cover, III, VI/VII, VIII), or by raising the little images of the Spirit Rider to expressive, sensitive, stylistically variegated emblems of the Bhil clans and the people of tribal and rural India.

The cow, sacred to the Hindus, and particularly the bull in the shape of Nandi, were given their immortal form in the various schools of sculpture of the Great Tradition. Thence their grandiose, weighty volumes descended, simplified and carved in stone or wood to the level of folk art (no. 99). They remain distinct from the primary geometry of the tribal-village art forms.[40]

In ancient times, in the third millennium B.C., the basic form of the bull, impetuously modelled (no. 1; plate IX), coexisted with its naturalistic shape, in Mohenjo-Daro. In a primary shape, the buffalo was found also in the ancient tombs of the Nilgiris of South India (no. 18).

On the level of village art, animal sculpture retains, though softened at times by descriptive naturalism (nos. 11, 12, 21), its basic, seemingly timeless cast. Ram, boar and elephant are created as if nourished on the same peaceful pasture (nos. 172, 173, 198, 200, 224). Stylistic varieties amongst these metal figurines, though slight, are yet sufficient to show the work of a definite region. But it requires a different technique like that of the Dhokra (nos. 228-251; plates XV, XVII, XVIII) and Kaser (nos. 147-149; plate X) figurines or a different material like pith (nos. 447-451) to allow the phantasy of the maker the invention of new skills and forms.

The figure of man in tribal and village art, connotes itself, it represents man as he is seen in the waking, dreaming and trance experience and given form by the artist. It represents preeminently his spirit, the Ancestor. The form of the ancestral spirit-figure, having the shape of man, peoples the tribal world of art. The anthropomorphic image of god was absent from it, originally.[41]

An unhewn stone marks the presence of deity. It is daubed with red colour which holds the memory of blood sacrifices. The stone is permanent. It outlasts the perishable, ever renewed offerings made by art. The stone is outside the temporality of man-shaped things.

Unhewn stones, placed under and canopied by the spreading branches of sacred trees are part of the Indian landscape. No conscious attempt is made at a harmonious arrangement. It comes about where the presence of deity is proffered by a visible though not man-made sign.

If the tribal and village art of India is seen against the high skyline of the Hindu temples with their countless images of gods, it is seen at the same time within the Indian landscape, which is dotted here and there, wherever you go, by a red-daubed stone, a sign of the presence of deity. While the presence of Aiyanar, the Lord, is marked, in principle, by a rough stone, the offerings, the works of art, small or gigantic, made of clay, proclaim his existence.

The tribal-village continuum of rural India extends, even today, into the towns as it must have at any other time. In the Harappan cities of the third millennium B.C., terra-cotta figurines abounded. They have tubular shapes or conical stumps for limbs, cylindrical or flattened bodies, faces pinched so that pellets for eyes can be affixed on either side of the nose (no. 2). Similar figurines are made today by the potters or the women of the village. According to the use that will be made of the clay figurines, they will be toys or, if consecrated, ritual objects. While some of the figurines are precise and subtle in proportions and contour (no. 356), others are sketchy (no. 22) or less competent in execution. But there are, besides these simple, basic types (nos. 3, 8, 9, 13), naturalistically modelled figurines (no. 14) and others whose faces are moulded (no. 4). Many layers and phases of art, tribal or urban, left their residues in these most ancient towns of the subcontinent, as they did subsequently in other cities.

Varieties of Tribal Art

In the tribal Nilgiri tombs, a funerary repertory of clay figurines is accommodated in a variety of types from the basic shapes of naturalistic intent of a buffalo (no. 18) to the seemingly sophisticated distortions of a "primitive" human figurine (nos. 16, 17). In the ancient city of Mathura, which the Greeks called "the city of the gods," a female figurine of primary abstract shape is assignable to the sixth century B.C. (no. 3); another, with her primary, three-dimensional shape flattened to a superhuman width of the hips, to the third century B.C. (no. 4). Her moulded face, however, shows a faint recollection of what could be implications of Greek art just leaving behind its archaic phase. This mother goddess, with her flattened width of hips, looks across space and time to a figurine from Patna (no. 13) of the second or third century A.D. Her basic form is that of a serpent above and woman below.

Primary, basic shapes underlay the complex charm of the ritual metal figurines of the Spirit Rider (nos. 25-34; plates XI-XIV, XVI). With less finesse and more immediacy the metal figurines of the tribal Kutiya Kond, on the Andhra – Orissa border, capture the movements of an animal, the way it stretches its neck, or those of young people in their insouciance (nos. 287-292; plate XXIV). Cruder technically than the Dhokra figurines discussed, they are related to them. The Kutiya Kond figurines are said to have been meant for the young bridegroom.[42] They were carried in the marriage procession and thus played their part in the sacrament of marriage. They are the most spontaneously animated of the tribal metal figurines. The animation is of two kinds for the planes of the figurines that are cast in wire-technique show this technique so that the airy texture of the surface with its raised, crossing or parallel lines not only directly encloses the core of the body but also suggestively models its volume. Here animal figurines generally are altogether encased in these meshes whereas the faces and thin limbs of human figures are without them and are modelled freely. The distortions of the latter make them appear agitated and tremulous. In Kond paintings, too—which were done only in dire necessity and were not ever meant to be looked at[43]—the limbs seem to bend and flicker. They are tossed by an excitement which, free from tragic motivation, found its expressive shape in the metal figurines. Compared with these, the figurines of the Spirit Riders are monumental and impersonal in their presence. They are directed forward towards one goal (nos. 25-34; plates XI-XIV, XVI). The Kutiya Kond figurines of animals and man, on the other hand, appear caught in the wilderness of life. Kond figurines are essentially three-dimensional; they lack the elegant silhouette of the figurines from Western India. The relation of the volumes of a Kond figurine is full of tension. This, together with the crudely spontaneous wire-technique, distinguishes the Kond figurines from those of Bastar with their ornately abstract shapes. Whereas the wire patterns, applied elsewhere in Orissa (no. 286) as well as in Bengal, Bihar and Bastar, on the smoothed metal ground are meticulous in their regularity and the straight lines of the wires, the Kond figurines wear their sheer wire net texture as if it were a loosely woven, tight-fitting web, its threads pulled this way and that way.

Few attempts have been made to study, on the spot, the different traditions of tribal art and to define their types of form.[44] The brass figurines differ in every tribe, yet in Mid-India they are always made by the same Hindu caste, the Kaser or Ghasia.[45] Though the caste remains the same, its members were mostly tribal converts. Each tribe would employ Ghasias who lived nearest to them and were their blood relatives. However, even the work of one and the same tribe may vary considerably. This is seen particularly where one and the same subject is represented.[46] Different degrees of Hinduization accrued on the underlying form or left it untouched. It would seem that Hinduization of tribal art increased from the fourteenth century. It was at that time that the Bhil lost the privilege to inaugurate the Rana of Mewar.[47]

A large group of diminutive metal images seems to have its centre of production to the south of the Bhil country, in the Deccan, around Nasik (Maharashtra).

While the images are sometimes those of Hindu gods, the form is of an archaic, tribal caste (nos. 165-172); the flat slab-like bodies of the figurines carry large heads, the faces projecting with a central peak, that of the nose. Blubber eyes bulge from the cheek slopes on either side of the nose bridge. These uniform, but plastically lively faces form a powerful accent above the puny, planar body. The bulk of the head, as in other tribal form traditions, proportionately exceeds and is here more massively three-dimensional than the rest of the figure. The limbs are tube-like extensions of the body. The figurines are frequently assembled in three-dimensional compositions. They are placed on a disc-shaped base (no. 166), or the base may be a long, narrow strip (no. 165). Each type of composition seems to be invented as the occasion demands, and in it the sprightly figures are distributed with zest. They completely exist in space, are freely placed within the spatial area. Truly three-dimensional group compositions are the exception in the Great Tradition of Indian sculpture which carves its images against the walls of the temple or observes a relief treatment even in the freestanding images of the temple sanctuary, as the image is meant to be seen essentially from the front only. The great South Indian bronzes of the Chola age, apart from the superb modelling of the figures, are timid or constrained in their arrangement when forming a group.[48] In the small figure-groups from Nasik, voids and masses interlock, each time in new rhythms and brisk patterns.

According to their ways of life, the tribes use art for specific purposes. The Santal of the Santal Parganas in Bihar occasionally use a carved litter *(rahi)* in which the bridal pair is carried (no. 264). This is not done by any other tribe. The carving of the litter enhances the effect of the procession which is part of the marriage rite. When a Santal craftsman begins his work on the litter, a pair of pigeons is sacrificed; when the litter is completed and its owner has taken possession, two more pigeons are part of another sacrifice. The activity of carving is part of the marriage rite, as is the procession of the marriage litter. The carvings, in low relief, are narrative: human figures in combined front-profile view, limbs at times overlapped in telling gestures and lively actions of spontaneously formed groups, and are based roughly on one groundline in common, in a cursive notation of figures, human and animal, more voluble and less expert but somehow paralleling Egyptian reliefs. The Santal, too, carve their one-stringed lutes or their fiddles, sometimes in the shape of woman, transfiguring the resonance of the instrument into rotundities known from Hindu sculpture and brought to the tribal level by the simplifications and distortions demanded by the shape of the instrument (no. 262; plate xxv). The prophetic head with its far-seeing inlaid eyes, traversed at the back by the tuning keys as a kind of ear-ornament, carried aloft on a neck of inordinate length, is a noble mask. Through its thin lipped mouth a god may speak—as he does through the dance-mask of another tribe, the Bhuiya (no. 153; plate xxx). Arms and hands closely hug the curved plane of the sounding-box body whose firmness is enhanced visually by the broad collar of the necklace (no. 262; plate xxv).

Sound and mask, the prophetic voice which speaks through mask and instrument, link auditory and visual experience in one manifestation of the numinous. The Saora tribe uses musical instruments in divination. The Oraon of Chota Nagpur regard musical instruments with something like religious awe.[49] With the Bhuiya, the gods speak prophetically through the mask while the wearer of the mask dances (nos. 153, 154; plate xxx). If the musical instrument, by means of the shape of the human figure, is transformed into an icon, the wearer of the mask loses his identity in the experience of the presence which the mask represents and shields.

Masks are made by the tribal people of Mid-India in assemblages of various materials and colours, in techniques ranging from matting to carving, and in styles from the abstract to grotesque exaggeration (nos. 153-158; plates xxx, xxxi), but with the sole exception of Verrier Elwin, no one has hitherto collected them. The tribal art of India, if collected at the beginning of this century, would have held its own in range and variety in comparison with that of Africa.[50] After that, where it has survived in its purity, it often shows its poverty (no. 152; plate xxv).

Where, smoothed to standards of Hindu art, the tribal proportions are followed, the directness of the underlying tribal form—even in its impoverished state—is lost (no. 145).

On the non-tribal level, and within Hinduism, Sannyasis perform ecstatic mask-dances during the Gambhira Festival of Shiva.[51] Before such an ascetic devotee puts on the wooden mask representing the deity which will take possession of him, he places the mask before the priest who performs the rite that brings life into it (*pranapratishtha*).

If the mask acts as façade for the temporal presence of the numinous in its wearer, it also protects him from contact with the direct glance of the outsider and makes him immune to the evil eye. In one of its particular usages, the mask (*chhau*) is worn by royal and other dancers of Seraikella in Bihar during the spring rites celebrating Nata Bhairava, the fearful form of Shiva, the Dancer[52] (no. 283). The *chhau* dance is integrally part of the worship of Shiva. The masks worn today with their blandly wistful, wide-eyed uniform beauty disengage the dancer's face from the emotion expressed by his body. They shield him from a reference of his art to his person. The *chhau* mask in its anonymity is an effective safeguard for the message of the dance conveyed by the movement of the body.

The mask (*mohra*) through which deity speaks is made of brass in the Kulu valley of the Western Himalayas (nos. 210-212). Each mask is a thanks-offering. It is consecrated by a priest (*pujari*) and the shaman talks through the mask answering the questions which have been put to the deity. The masks of the gods are attached to and piled high on a chariot and taken out in procession. Each village has its own masks of the Goddess and her attendant divinities. From their high position on the mountain of the chariot, they inspect the harvest.

These masks of deity, unlike those worn by men, are kept from year to year in the village as property of the deity. A tithe is collected for the preparation of new masks. The money is paid to the craftsmen through the clerk of the village. In this rural setup, the voice of the Goddess is made manifest by its mouthpiece, the mask. The brass masks of the Kulu valley are plaques showing the crowned head of the Goddess and terminating horizontally below the breast. An ancient mask of the ninth to tenth century[53] is cast in a shape belonging to the Great Tradition of Indian sculpture of that phase. It is the work of a master who must have been chosen for this task by the king who ruled over Kulu. More recent masks are without the opulent, classically formulated naturalism of the great Indian, early mediaeval tradition. A planar "chest" plaque showing as a rule, a necklace formed of a pair of serpents, symbols of fertility, and a mere suggestion of breasts in very low relief, extends below the mask of the crowned face, moulded in high relief and carrying, at times, an aeginetan smile, on its once classical and now schematized features.

Metal and votive plaques accompany the history of the Great Tradition of Indian art.[54] Concurrently and earlier the tribal use of the mask must have been established in India as it was elsewhere since the time of the Cave of the Sorcerer.

The Kulu masks, while looking out on the harvest, look back to a past where metal plaques were given as offerings to the gods, where masks were worn so that the voice of the gods could be heard and where images were made of the gods portraying their ideal beauty. Three different traditions met and helped to create the locally circumscribed Kulu mask. Its isolated survival may indicate an entry of the anthropomorphic image of deity into sculpture by way of the mask as it also shows an appropriation from the Great Tradition of Indian sculpture and its transformation to rural needs and practice.

The Kulu mask (nos. 210-212) and the Nasik group compositions and figurines are each the result of an application to rural practice of the Great Tradition of

Indian sculpture. In the Nasik compositions it frequently lent its iconography, though not its manner, to the directional relationship of shapes contained within the volume of one spatial area (nos. 165, 166, 172). In the Kulu valley, it imbued with its own tradition of form an already complex type of a tribal-rural past.

The tribal art of Mid-India, however, retained its identity in each of the tribal units. If they adopted Hindu symbolism as the Gond did in carving their marriage booths, each post representing a palace of many storeys such as that in which Hindu and Buddhist gods are seen to dwell,[55] the figures shown and the stories enacted on the Gond carvings are more closely related to the wall paintings of the Gond, Saora and other tribes than they are to the representations carved in stone, long ago, on Buddhist and Hindu monuments.[56] At some points, Hindu concepts and symbols such as that of the palace of the gods, were adapted by the tribes.[57] At some point, however, craftsmen of tribal extraction contributed their style to monuments of the Great Tradition.

Funerary posts, megalithic or carved in wood, belong not only to the tribal cultures of Middle India. They are set up in rural Bengal to this day, and even in the suburbs of the city of Calcutta[58] (no. 332). These *brisakat (vrishakashta)*, or "wooden bull posts," show the post transformed into a general likeness of the deceased, man or woman, young or old, whose head is crowned by a "palace" architecture, housing in its first storey the figure of a bull, the symbol of righteousness *(dharma)*, and that of a Shiva-linga in its top storey, the bull being here the means of attaining the highest goal, the domain of Shiva. The ancestral effigy carries as its superstructure an image of Shivaite hopes. Reduced to the bare outlines of form and meaning, such posts are carved today by an old woman sculptor in a crowded street of Calcutta. They are set up near a pond and are left to decay, uncared for, a year after a death has occurred.

From the Spirit Riders of the Bhil and other tribes, such as the Korku, from the horses of Aiyanar in South India, and those of uncounted village gods throughout the country to the hobbyhorse ridden by a devotee of Shiva in West Bengal,[59] the work of art was an instrument of communication with the realm of the spirit, the other world. Its form was a creative outcome of the experience of that world. It functioned as a support for wishes and as the only guarantee for their fulfillment. The work of art here fills the void of all that is not within reach and which must be postulated and hoped to be achieved, be it mere wish fulfillment, a feeling of security or the realization in this life of a state beyond it.

Differently located in the creative atmosphere is the art of the Naga tribes (nos. 452-467; plate XXIII). The work of art made by a Naga serves as a repository of magical virtue, of power which leads to achievement and success. The Naga who live on the northeast frontier of India belong to the Tibeto-Burman family of man. They are a group by themselves, unrelated to the other tribal people of India. They number in all about four hundred thousand, but fall into distinct tribes whose art is linked to their entire social structure. Art with them is a ritual of magic fraught with danger. The artist must prepare himself, restrict his diet and be chaste before he starts his work.[60] If he breaks one of the rules, he may die.

Some of the Naga are, or were, headhunters. According to them, that part of a man which is his magical virtue adheres to the skull, the other part goes to the land of the dead.[61] The Konyak Naga—some of whom are expert sculptors[62]—carry around their necks tallies of the heads of those they killed in warfare. These are made of wood or brass (no. 461).[63] In Naga sculpture, the virtue which was in the living, man or animal, seems transferred, as it were, into its created form, where this virtue is enhanced by the ability of the craftsman to do so in creating form.[64] The art of representation is here felt to be a dangerous transmutation, an act of creative magic, for which the artist must brace and discipline his person.

The artist, like the other Naga, here is a warrior. He carves the main pillar of the village dormitory of the men *(morung)* and its open porch, and the houses of the donors of the Feasts of Merit. He represents animals, real or fantastic ones, warriors, couples, human and animal, dancing couples, tigers or frogs eating the moon. The figures are to be effective: the tigers will make the boys ferocious, the elephants will make them strong, the hornbills will make them fertile. Magically their virtue has gone into their representation and acts on the beholder. This metempsychosis-like transmutation through the medium of art is the Naga contribution to the relation of the artist to his object and to the beholder.

The *morung,* which is the setting of the Feasts of Merit, and the ritual bamboo mugs *(chunga)* from which the rice-beer is drunk, are decorated with death-shapes, floating and depleted (nos. 462-467). Today we see only the end of the Feast of Merit, the end of Naga life as it had been lived. Headhunting now being forbidden, art with the Naga has lost its raison d'être. Even before that, the carvings of the ritual drinking-mugs of the Phom do not differ greatly in quality from the carvings by the great Ang, the sacred chief of his Konyak village,[65] and by his two brothers. They show an almost conscious stylization where slender, weightless figures look like phantoms, suspended in afterthoughts.

The three-dimensional wooden or clay figures (no. 452), the latter carved like wood, and particularly the wooden grave effigies, however, are free from the decorator's touch (nos. 452-456, 458-460; plate xxiii). They are set up for the warriors and other important persons for the habitation of their spirit. To the Naga, they are "live" images as long as the spirit dwells in them, but after the proper rites have been performed, the image ceases to be "live" and can be thrown away. Whether severally blocked out in rectilinear planes or more tubular in shape, whether grave effigies or not, the more abstract among the figures are three-dimensional patterns of pathos. It speaks differently from each sculpture, from eyes and mouth which are assimilated to each other. Their three circles, or three slits, intensify an underlying mood. Choice and place of ear-ornaments, coloured fibres or cheap buttons, enliven the identity of each figure or group,[66] whatever its style (no. 456; plate xxiii). It may rely on geometric shapes which, though static, cohere by tensions generated by their contrast, or on a relationship of sinuous surface planes and spaces gliding between tenuously defined volumes.

The motivation for decorating the Naga *morung* and the houses of the donors of the Feasts of Merit, or in the case of the warrior himself, his own person, is the enhancement of life to which the experience of death contributes its share. The work of art, here, is the form given to the meeting of man and the supernatural, of man and the special power, which is not usually or normally his own—and for which the Naga has to kill an enemy or tiger. The artist contributes his work as a part of the total rite of living; it is his function or duty to do so.

He does not always do this willingly. Amongst the Kond, whose young men of one tribal unit, the Kutiya Kond, take pleasure in the small brass figurines made by the Ghasia, "no one paints unless he has to, and nearly every picture has behind it a history of tragedy and sorrow which it was designed to cure."[67] The lively and sometimes tormented line of the small figures in Kond paintings follows a pattern seen in a dream.[68] "Once made, no one ever looks at the painting." Here, apart from the artist himself, even the temporary beholder—who takes part in the funerary rites performed by means of the ancestral image, which then is thrown away—is excluded. The work of art is created and effective between the supernatural and the artist alone. The Kond practice art as self-therapy. They are sceptical about success. "Often the gods change their minds and send dreams demanding that the painting should be rubbed out and a new one prepared."

The Art Ritual of Women

1 Magic Diagrams

The surface for a painting, as a rule, is vertical; if it is horizontal it will be a ceiling
or the ground. Classical antiquity had use for pictorial mosaic floors. India knew
floor paintings *(dhuli-chitra)*[69] and to this day they are executed on the ground,
mainly with white rice paste but also with coloured powders. They are painted in
tribal societies as magical diagrams, in different colours.[70] The magic function of art,
in India, is vested in the diagrams, primarily drawn on the floor.

The art of painting on the floor, in rural India, is the prerogative of women. Its
traditions are handed down from mother to daughter. Her training begins in her
fifth or sixth year and she reaches competence in her twelfth year. A non-Brahman
priest may be engaged at times. The art of painting on the floor is non-Brahman
though it can be practiced by Brahman women. The women learned it ultimately
from traditions more ancient than those of the Aryan Brahmans, and they elaborated
them in forms by which the floor is covered with the magic potency in patterns
peculiar to each part of India. The material itself of these magic diagrams, the rice
powder, is felt to have magical powers. So is the copper which formed part of the
substance of the Bhil Spirit Riders. Rice powder acts magically. It scares away evil
spirits.[71] The designs drawn with it on the floor have magical power. They are
essentially diagrams. Within the confines, within the more or less intricate geometrical
lines of the diagram an invoked presence finds its allotted place. Its power is confined
and thereby held in its place and for the purpose for which the diagram was drawn.
The magic diagram makes it possible for power to be present and it brings this
presence into the power of the person who has made the diagram. Apart from
diagrams drawn by women, *yantras,* or magical diagrams are, also, part of Tantrik
Hindu practice.[72] A mandala is such a magic diagram. Mandalas were widely used in
Tantrik Buddhism. They determine the composition of one of the most characteristic
and elaborate types of Buddhist paintings.[73] Tantriks who make a *yantra* have to
avoid food prepared by women and even the sound of a woman's bangles.[74] Is it
partly because they have to guard their art from those who had the power to evolve it?
The meaning of a *yantra* goes far beyond that of diagrams drawn by women.

The floor designs drawn mostly freehand by women with rice paste or powder on
the earthen ground range from geometrical diagrams by themselves to their
association with other symbols such as footprints—which are those of the Great
Goddess. These spellbinding configurations are known under many names, such as
kolam, mandana, aripana, according to the style and region in which they were
evolved.[75] Originally far removed from decoration, all these ritual magic designs are
forms of a will directed to an end which is to confine and control a supernatural
power and to isolate it from the ground. The effect of these symbolic shapes is at
one with their efficacy. They do not form abstract patterns for they are the shape
of conceptions. They are intuited and functional diagrams transmitted by women.

Some of these designs are drawn every morning or in the evening; others at each
sacrament of life *(samskara)*, at the passage from one state of life to another.
They are drawn at the birth of a child, at the boy's investiture with the sacred thread,
and at the time of marriage. Others are drawn as acts of devotion when taking
a vow *(vrata)* to achieve a desired result. These are drawn on certain days of the
year of special significance in the course of the sun.

The *vrata alpona*[76] and *aripana* are richest in design and connotation. The
sun, the moon, the stars, the earth are integrated in them and also the things desired
by the young girl who draws them, ornaments, a mirror and the like; and the
whole cosmos is conjured up to bless and fulfill a young girl's wish—for even a simple
wish is not to be fulfilled if no effort is made at the right time to communicate
with the powers that work in heaven and on earth. Here it is the magic circle, in

other designs the sacred square, a concatenation of curves or an intersection of polygons, that encloses the magic field. Into it the power of a god is invoked. It is assigned to its enclosure, it is spellbound. It cannot escape; it is controlled. It is held in its confinement, bound in the plane by the outline of the enclosure so that it cannot escape into the ground where, like lightning, it would be rendered impotent.[77]

The most ancient Sanskrit treatise on Indian painting prescribes the worship of the Sun God through an eight-petalled lotus flower drawn on the ground.[78] Several other Puranas[79] speak of the art of drawing the sun on the ground and that the sun was worshipped in a circle in early days.[80] However, this practice was not sanctioned by the Vedas;[81] it belonged to those outside the Vedic pale. The drawing of a magic diagram on the floor however became essential in building a Hindu temple.

The power of the supernatural is believed magically to be controlled and made effective at a given spot and time. The art of floor painting is a visual form of magic, a delineation and coercion of the presence of the numinous. Its diagrams avoid becoming stereotyped, they are enriched and evolve where, as in the *vrata alpona* of Eastern India, the hopes and wishes of the artist are precipitated into the design on the floor.

2 Kantha Textiles

Allied to the *vrata alpona* is the textile art of the *kantha* (nos. 414-445; plates XLI, XLV and colour plates XXXVIII, XXXIX, XLIII, XLVI-XLVII). The *kantha*,[82] a patched cloth, was made mainly in Eastern Bengal (East Pakistan), but also in Bihar, of worn-out and disused saris and dhotis. Their thin, white cotton cloth with its coloured borders, when getting threadbare, was cut, patched, quilted and embroidered. According to the thickness of the quilt and its size, it was used as a cover to be spread, as a wrap to be worn, or folded as a bag. The white ground of the quilt was embroidered and reinforced with coloured threads drawn from the coloured borders. The colours of the *kanthas* of the early part of the nineteenth century are mainly red and blue; in the later half of the century, yellows and greens, particularly linden green, are also included. The material of the *kanthas* are rags and their threads. Joined afresh, these tatters are given a new wholeness. Their embroidered designs spring from this meaning. The *kantha* is a work which gives wholeness to things that were of no use any more, to fragments without any significance. This rite of the restitution of wholeness is a domestic one, performed by women, though rarely by Brahman women. The more ornate *kanthas* are the work of Kayastha, or middle-class, women from the homes of clerks and scribes, though women of all castes and classes of the rural population, including Muslim women, had, or embroidered *kanthas*. They were given as presents within the family or to friends.

Textile symbolism in India is hallowed by tradition. In the Rig Veda and the Upanishads, the universe is envisioned as a fabric woven by the gods. The cosmos, the ordered universe, is one continuous fabric with its warp and woof making a grid pattern.[83] Hence the importance of wholeness, not only of the uncut garment, like the sari or the dhoti, but also of the cloth woven all in one piece, on which a sacred picture is to be painted.[84] Whether as cover for the body or as ground for a painting, the uncut fabric is a symbol of totality and integrity. It symbolizes the whole of manifestation. Inversely, rags are offered to the gods. Chindiyadeo, the Lord of Tatters, gives a new whole cloth if a rag is offered to him. There are rag shrines all over the country. Their goddess is Chithariya Bhavani, Our Lady of Tatters.[85] The Buddha wore a patchwork robe *(sanghati)*. Some of the reliefs of the Mathura school of the second century A.D. show him thus clad. Lord Chaitanya (1485-1533), the apostle and visionary, draped in a *kantha* the ecstasies which overwhelmed his body.[86] The colourful patchwork of the robes of saints forms part of miniature paintings of the Mughal period. The patched robe of the Buddha or of a saint

belongs to him in his nature of Saviour. The rags are given a new wholeness.
They clothe holiness.

Clothes being worn near the body are part of its ambience and are personal. Should
an enemy get hold of any bit of the cloth he might practice black magic against the
former wearer.[87] The patchwork quilt, a collection of tatters, guarantees immunity
from black magic, protection and security, as do even the rags themselves when
offered to the gods.

The symbolism inherent in the patchwork of the *kantha* is the ground which is
embroidered with nearly equal perfection on both sides.[88] The act of making-whole
demands perfection throughout. The design is drawn by the embroiderer herself
or by another woman. It is neither the work of a professional artist nor is it copied
from anywhere. No two *kanthas* are ever alike; each is an original creation, although
kanthas from one and the same district follow certain types and these have more
in common than those from villages at a greater distance.

The design of the square or rectangular field of the *kantha,* in principle, relies
on a central circle occupied by a lotus flower. Four trees mark the four corners.
The central, wide-open, many-petalled lotus is an ancient Indian symbol of universal
manifestation and of this world in particular. The four trees are symbols of the
four directions; their meaning stems from Mesopotamia. The disc of the
many-petalled lotus, when drawn as *alpona,* on the floor, would support a vessel
filled with water, in the centre. Deity is invoked and known to be present in a
vessel filled with water. In the design of the *kantha,* the central lotus is inscribed in a
square. The entire ground of the quilted cloth between the lotus and the directional
trees is filled with figures, objects, symbolic devices and scenes whose shapes and
combinations are dictated by the imagination of the artist. Themes from ancient
myths and legends are laid out next to scenes and figures commenting on
contemporary life, and both are permeated with purely symbolic devices. The design
of the *kanthas* provides wide margins for showing the contents of a woman's mind.
Their figures and symbols are freely associated and rhythmically assembled.
In some *kanthas,* the figures are those of animals only. A Muslim *kantha,* faithful to
the precepts of a non-iconic art, shows nothing but scrollwork (no. 419). On the
underlying central and directional composition of the *kantha,* as its framework,
is displayed the personality of the embroiderer. It shows not only in the planar
composition but also in the selection of themes from the common reservoir of the
tradition as it is lived by her at the moment of her needlework, but especially in the
selection and spacing of the stitches and the resulting texture and form of
the embroidery.

The stitches are of the simplest kind, the running stitch being not only the main
but also the most ingeniously employed. According to the length and spacing of the
single stitches, they circumscribe, and, this is their truly creative function, they
organize a surface in a multitude of small squares and triangles so that its speckled
texture of ground and embroidery is light or dense with colours. Closely parallel
running stitches give a more gliding quality to the ground cover which they produce.
Both of these modes and their combinations filling a given surface are bounded
by a continuous line which the back-stitch yields. Within its firm contour, be it red
or blue, the running stitches, according to their density, not only produce different
colour values, but together with a particular texture of the surface, they give a
tonality of its own to each *kantha.* Moreover, they are conducted so as to produce an
effect of modelling of its own kind on the textured surface. Modelling by means
of running stitches appears to be an invention of the embroiderers of the *kanthas.*
It is a purely textile equivalent of modelling with brush and colours. In this,
the "classical" tradition of Indian painting, as in Ajanta, excelled. Visualization
in terms of the modelled form, an irrepressible sense of plasticity, are essentially
Indian. This age-old and "classical" Indian quality was given form by textile means
in the art of the *kantha* of East Bengal in the nineteenth century. The effect of

68

modelling is produced by the closely spaced rows of stitches running parallel with the outline of a figure. This brings about an area of uniform texture and tone. Toward the interior of the outlined surface, density and direction of the stitches change, producing other areas set off from their neighbour zones. This, together with the speckled textural effect of the stitches which leads the eyes in more than one direction, also yields effects akin to op art but having representational intentions. The op art effect is bounded by the outline of the respective figure of elephant or horse.

The figures of the *kantha*, "modelled" by these colourful stitches which allow the white ground to shine through, are also foreshortened and their limbs may overlap without, however, their giving the effect of any spatial context. The figures are scattered rhythmically over the white ground and if limbs or figures overlap, their area is part of the embroidered ground, for though the figure may be modelled in terms of stitching, the modelling has no substance to it. It suggests volume by directional movement. Far from creating an illusion of the body, its embroidered form is dematerialized (nos. 433, 435, 443; plate XLV and colour plates XLIII, XLVI, XLVII). Often the figures are shown in a contraction of front and profile. At other times, an x-ray view allows one to see across them. As an outcome of this, some *kanthas* create their own figures, having the shape of a man, with or without a body, the number of limbs also being at the discretion of the artist. This, though, does not refer to their multiplicity which iconography may postulate in the case of the figures of deities but to their reduction, to stumps instead of limbs, contraction of two limbs into one, or omission of one limb or the other according to the needs of identification, rhythm and compositional clarity (no. 443; plate XLV and colour plate XLIII).

By the middle of the century, the embroidery stitch is more frequently resorted to than it was earlier. It adds more compact areas and stronger hues to the *kantha*. But these stronger accents too sink into the ground of the *kantha*. The ground between figures, as often as not, is reinforced all over with stitches running in closely set parallels around each figure. For this, white thread is used and, less frequently, blue or red thread. These colours give a pointilistically muted tonality to the vibrant texture of the ground of *kanthas* assignable to the turn of the century.

Thematically, the art of the *kantha* is an enriched textile version of the art of the *aripana* or *alpona,* the painting on the floor, its magic purpose being enhanced by the textile symbolism of its material and the way this is used. Stylistically, its form is entirely its own, adjusting an ancient propensity of India's classical art to its own textile and planar sensibilities.

The art of the *kantha* is a rural art. While it is imbued with Hindu myths, it is also perceptive of the life of India in the nineteenth century with some of its manners and fashions derived from those of the West, an imaginative blend of the actuality of living where every day contributes some novelty to be absorbed by the stream of the tradition and integrated into its style. It is an art of leisure. Sophisticatedly primitive, the quilt of the *kantha* integrates many layers of the fabric of Indian life, tribal as well as urban, in its conception. The magic that underlies its purpose is that of love—not of coercion, as that of the diagrammatic floor drawings whose purpose is wish fulfillment. A *kantha* is given as a present, it is conceived with an outgoing mind and brings the entire personality of the maker to the person for whom it is made. Its composition is a ritual being laid out around the centre of the lotus of manifestation. Its symbols have universal validity in the four directions. To their whirls and waves, to the lotus and the life trees are assigned the innumerable figured scenes of the mythic, ever-present past together with episodes of the passing scene.

All of them are firmly stitched into a reconstituted, vibrant wholeness. The *kantha* is the form, by textile means, of a creative process of integration within each woman who makes a *kantha*.

Succumbing to the, in India, belated effects of the Industrial Revolution, the art of the *kantha* died after the first quarter of the twentieth century. It is not known when this art began. Its upsurge in a narrowly circumscribed area has not its like elsewhere. *Kanthas* from Bihar are without the wealth of associated content and textile imagination (nos. 280-282). Although made in the same technique, their widely spaced design is an adaptation, in terms of embroidery, of the staid, placid lines of a certain type of painting of Bihar. The Bengali *kanthas* resemble a form of painting in Bengal only insofar as their overall character stems from the magic art of the *alpona*. As much as the South Indian sanctuaries, teeming with their hundreds of clay horses, clay cattle and clay human figures offered in sacred groves express in their form the mystery of autochthony, the *kanthas* of East Bengal (East Pakistan) are saturated with and express a numinous power, the *shakti* of this region, working through its women and given form by innumerable disciplined stitches. Both these forms of art, that of the South Indian half-Brahman priest-potter and that of the Bengali Hindu matron—it was the older women, as a rule, who made the *kanthas*—represent traditional village art in fulfillment of rites of offering.

3 Painting

Women in other parts of India have their own inherited traditions of painting. Not only the respective diagrams on the floor are their prerogative. In Mithila, in North Bihar, the women of Brahman families and those of the Kayastha, or middle class, paint the walls of their homes for the celebration of two of the major sacraments of life.[89] With them, moreover there is no significant transition within the life of man that is not marked by an *aripana* on the floor. The paintings act as projections of the meaning of that moment on floor and walls around the person when the rites are performed. Some of the sacraments bound to be observed in each generation are: birth, marriage, the investiture with the sacred thread in the upper castes, and also the first haircut or the piercing of the earlobes. The Maithil wall paintings, done for the sacred thread ceremony and for weddings, have their standard repertory of images, painted according to the stylistic variations peculiar to each social group.[90] Symbols from the *aripana* or floor diagrams—which are particularly rich in motifs in Mithila—occur also in the wall paintings amidst a generally figural setting. As in the art of the *kantha*, freely associated scenes and figures are part of an organized composition whose units, within their precise outlines, seem to float on the white ground of the wall. The women also paint on paper recurrent standard types of figures and compositions of the paintings on the walls (nos. 256-261; plates XXXVII, XLIV). Their distortions commend themselves to eyes familiar with expressive and geometrical form. The paintings on the walls are more permanent than are the floor paintings whose dried rice paste or coloured dust last only for the occasion, are trodden on—dust which has been trodden on has mystical powers[91]—and wiped off. The wall paintings decay in less than ten years, and then the time has come for new ones.

The domestic art of the Maithil wall paintings follows the pictorial traditions of the family and caste to which the painter belongs—whereas the textile art of the *kantha* precipitates into a given frame of reference the inner world and psychic tensions of its maker. It is the most personal form of a traditional, ritual and domestic village art.

In the Maithil wall paintings which may or may not be confined within a frame or border, the figures are evenly distributed over the area to which they adhere with a clear colour spread within the circumscribing drawing. Its representational function is simplified, its quality is that of a cognizance not far from toyland. The rhythms however, of the work of Kayastha women in spacing the single elements are akin to those of tribal paintings. There they are urgent and stark. Here the single elements are stylized.

All the same, the aspects of tribal and village art hitherto described were imbued with the magic of ritual necessity and fitness. They belonged to a large part to non-Brahmanic and non-Hindu traditions. These visually conceived and executed rites were performed generally by specialized practitioners, like the South Indian Kusavan potter-priests and by women trained to celebrate the visual rites and who, inasmuch as they created form, were artists.

While the women of Mithila celebrate in their paintings the sacraments of the life of man, peasant women in villages of the Panjab, around Delhi, in parts of Uttar Pradesh and Rajasthan celebrate the sacraments of the cosmos; in seasonal rites the Great Mother, under different names and shapes, is made to inhabit her image, which is the work of the village women during the days when the rites are performed before it. The image of the goddess Hoi, whose body is the square diagram of the cosmos, is assimilated to the shape of man by adding to the square a head and the extremities, or also to that of a house in which man has his dwelling or to both at the same time. The image is painted on a wall of a house in the village. When, however, the Great Goddess as Sanjhi is made to dwell in her image, her shape is a composition of triangles entirely covered with multiform and star-shaped clay discs. They are applied to a coating of mud and cow dung, which is given to an outer wall of a house (plate XXVIII). The small clay elements painted white and speckled with orange, blue and yellow, cover, a starry array, the dark, triangulated shape of the Goddess. She is accompanied by the small figure of her brother who brings offerings to her on the eighth of the Navaratri rites of nine nights, when his image is added to that of the Great Goddess. On the tenth day the entire painted relief is removed from the wall which now is painted white and the figure of a peacock is drawn on it, while the remnants of the image are drowned in the village pond.[92] Unique in their technique of relief appliqué and painting, the Sanjhi representations made by peasant women form part of the visual-tactile creativeness of rural India which in Western India combines not only the effect of mirrors and textiles but of mirrors and mud wall in patterns as free and disciplined as those produced by the stitches of *kanthas*.

Rural Practice and the Great Tradition

The specialized and professional artist or craftsman belonging to the Hindu tradition worked for a patron in village or town, or for tribal people, or was dependent on an urban public.

Scroll paintings are the work of professional craftsmen *(chitrakara)*. They were exhibited in ancient times, for they are mentioned by Pantanjali in the middle of the second century B.C.[93] The long, vertical scroll paintings from West Bengal and Bihar are narrative (nos. 265-279, 366-387; plates XXXII, XXXIII) and thus different from the configurations of the floor and wall paintings of village and tribal art. Their compositions are akin to the complex majority of the carved panels of the corner posts of the Bharhut railing of the second century B.C. which appear to be lithic versions, in relief, of scroll paintings. The practice of painting vertical scrolls has mainly survived in West Bengal and in the Santal Parganas, Bihar, whereas large, horizontal scroll paintings (no. 41) but also vertical ones (no. 40) come from Rajasthan. The painters in Bengal belong in the main to the painter caste *(chitrakara)*.[94] An ancient text accounts for the low status of the painters. They fell from grace as their paintings transgressed the Brahmanic instructions. They were not painted according to hieratic rules and were therefore defective.[95] This story wants to account for the low status of the *chitrakaras,* to which they had fallen by the thirteenth century. Another community of painters in Bengal are the *jadu-patuas*[96] (no. 271, cf. no. 369). They are itinerant aboriginal mendicants, "Hindu" magicians, brassworkers and painters. They paint for the tribal Santal. Their name, *jadu-patua,* means "magic-painter." Their styles and also those of the paintings of *chitrakaras* working for the Santal are, on the whole, nearer to tribal brevities (nos. 265, 269, 270, 378) than is the opulence of the various Bengali styles

of the other *chitrakaras* (nos. 366, 368, 379, 380, 382-384, 387; plate xxxii).
Though *chitrakaras* are specialized craftsmen, some of them work in several media.
The *chitrakaras,* or painters, often also model in clay. However, they are trained as
painters and gain proficiency by painting on the walls of their houses. These
exercises are rubbed off daily.[97] Their scrolls were painted in gouache originally,
it would seem, on cloth, and subsequently on paper mounted on cloth.

Tribal and village traditions commingle in the painted scrolls. The various schools
represented by paintings from different centres carry on each the style created by
a local master painter. Some of the early scrolls (ca. 1800) show an awareness
of Rajput and Mughal types though these are recast consistent with a deeper
tonality, avoidance of suggestions of the third dimension and a calmly flowing line
(no. 366). Scrolls painted in Hooghly call to mind qualities of Etruscan painting[98]
(no. 367; plate xxxiii). Later in the nineteenth and in the twentieth century,
different "schools" can be localized. The burnt sienna and indigo blue tonality of
scrolls from Manbhum, Purulia, West Bengal (nos. 385, 386), holds pent-up
emotion packed in dense, contiguous compositions floating in broad, curvilinear
rhythms. This "school" is easily distinguished from the archaic, arrested gestures,
tensely planar composition and strong, quiet colours of the Hooghly paintings (no.
367; plate xxxiii) or from the lyrical, voluble style of many degrees, on white or red
ground of the Midnapur paintings where large figures crown the scroll[99] (nos. 379,
380, 384; plates xxxii). The subjects painted illustrate Hindu myths. A cycle
which kept its popularity over the last thousand years and more are the *yama patas,*
the paintings of the rewards of good and evil to be experienced in the realm of
Yama, the Lord of Death.[100]

The scroll paintings *(pata)* were exhibited by the painters who acted as picture
showmen and bards at the same time. They recited a passage from scripture and
legend while pointing to the respective picture on the scroll, depicting in successive
panels the relevant passages. The *pata* or *pat* was hung up on a bamboo frame, the
rest of the scroll being rolled up, and the particular incident was displayed which a
passerby needed for his edification. The painter-bards on the crossroads are no longer
part of the Bengal scene. While their art, in the early twentieth century, borders on
religious folk art (no. 387), the *jadu-patuas* practice magic *(jadu)* through some
of their paintings (nos. 370-372). These they paint for the tribal Santal. The
painter comes with his ready-made schematic portraits of which one or the other is
bound to fit the type of the recently dead amongst the tribal Santal whose house
he visits. The dead are believed to wander blindly in the other world until the
jadu-patua gives them eyesight by painting the eyes in the "portrait." These
"portraits" painted for the Santal are distinguished from the work of the *chitrakaras*
by their economy of colours. The scroll paintings intended for Santal audiences,
however, lack the relaxedly flowing lines and also the rich warm colours of the
Bengali scroll paintings. Their colours are generally light and cool; their crudely
vehement economy of line is nearer to tribal wall paintings in Middle India than
to the residual opulence of the Bengali village styles.

The paintings done for the Santal represent the tribal tradition amongst the rural
painters, the *chitrakaras* and *jadu-patuas* of Eastern India,[101] while the *patuas,* who
practiced their calling near the Kali Temple in Kalighat—which is now part of
Calcutta—produced their pictures for the pilgrims and visitors, many of whom came
from Calcutta (nos. 388-413; plate xxxiv). Originally, the *patuas* of Kalighat
worked in wood. Then they made clay images of Hindu gods to be worshipped at
their annual festivals. In between, they painted and made clay and wooden toys.[102]

The paintings particularly associated with them are in watercolour on millmade
sheets of paper. They are religious but also satirical in content. They also translate
into their own style natural objects, plants, fruits, animals, following the example of
the British in India who had been fascinated by the Indian flora and fauna.
Kalighat paintings have been called "bazaar paintings,"[103] for they could be bought

by anyone and for very little. Made for the man in the street, they supplied him with images he could take home, images which appealed to him on many levels. And they did more than that.

Kalighat paintings translate the narrative style of the village *patuas* into a new monumentality. It owes as much to the classical tradition of Indian painting, as practiced in Ajanta—whose ample fluid curves had glided along an unbroken though weakened chain from master to pupil into the linearized context of the scroll paintings—as it owes to Western classicism brought to Calcutta by the British. Kalighat paintings, at the height of their style in the last quarter of the nineteenth century, condense silhouette and modelling of the figures in sweeping outlines of the continuous brush strokes themselves. The paintings and brush drawings are monumental in their presentation on an otherwise mostly blank page (nos. 390, 395, 397; plate xxxiv). Preceding the work of Matisse, some of the brush drawings prefigure it (nos. 390, 391; plate xxxiv). Out of Indian tradition and impressions of Western painting, the "bazaar" painters, descendants of low-caste and hereditary craftsmen created forms as valid as, and akin to, some of the later work by leading artists in the West. In the Kalighat brush drawings of the later nineteenth century, moreover, old slumbering memories of creativeness seem actualized. Sinuosities which had ripened in Indian sculpture in the sixth century and dilated the potent shapes of the Goddess in even a humble offering plaque from the Himalayan foothills or the Panjab in the eighth century (no. 189; plate xxxv), sustain the sweep of line of the Kalighat drawings (no. 390; plate xxxiv).

Kalighat paintings are an outcome of the residual Great Tradition of Indian painting and of a local, traditional village art and their spontaneous transformation when exposed to currents of Western art active in the nearby city of Calcutta in the nineteenth century (no. 365). Some of the *kanthas* show the opposite process, on a different level, by integrating city fashions and foreign types into the rural atmosphere and closely stitched context of their embroidered field.

An altogether different phenomenon however is the form of Jagannatha, carved in wood and painted (nos. 293, 294, 300, 308). The image is set up in its traditional and repeatedly renewed shape in the Temple of Jagannatha, the Lord of the World, in Puri, Orissa.

There, to the south of Bengal, on the east coast, a miraculous thing happened when, according to legend, a log of wood was seen floating in the sea and a mythical king ordered a carpenter to make it into an image of God. The carpenter stipulated that he be left working behind closed doors for twenty-one days. The king opened the door prematurely; the carpenter, who was God himself, vanished. Though the image remained incomplete, it was installed in the temple.[104] The image of Jagannatha, Lord of the World—in his temple of the twelfth century in Puri, an imposing structure built in the Great Tradition and of lavish sophistication —is a log of wood. Just that and nothing else. Large eyes are painted on it and arm stumps branch out. In megalithic cultures, a log of wood is a proxy for a piece of stone, which, in tribe and village, was set up to indicate the presence of deity. The Uriya legend speaks of a miracle that happened when a primeval shape came to be the centre of the most meticulously ordained rites of orthodox Hindu worship. The image of Jagannatha stares open-eyed from paintings and wooden images of Orissa. Around it grew an iconographic style of painting entirely its own, a temple-craft based on tribal tradition. Its reverberations were felt in Bengal (no. 385).

An irruption of a stark shape of tribal art into the Great Tradition is not the rule. It is generally that shapes of the Great Tradition, such as its costumes, are accepted beyond the centres of its activity. Within a feudal society, its many princely and lesser courts and patrons, art had a wide public, the same rural public which listened to their favourite ballads and to the recitation of the sacred myths. The wisdom of India was transmitted orally and visually, written texts were resorted to only when

73

memory had become weakened. Visual transmission was relied upon far more than the written word. The making and beholding of symbols and images were part of living. In Bengal and Bihar, the bard-and-showman exhibited his long scrolls with their neatly divided horizontal panels, each illustrating a phase of the story. In Rajasthan, he showed his wide, horizontal scroll, its composition one overall tessellated field of figures, telling the story of Pabuji, the Rathore chief, and his coal-black mare.[105] One recognises the Mewar school of painting but only as far as figures and costumes go. The style of the Pabuji paintings has a planar coherence and epic width unknown to the "miniature" paintings of the Mewar school (no. 41).

Feudal styles and temple traditions, variously blended, sunk into the fabric of the local practice of art, as it renewed itself celebrating the rites of the seasons in nature and those in the life of man. A series of paintings from Paithan, in Maharashtra, in Mid-India, lays out its epic and mythical themes in a restrainedly heroic manner (nos. 177-181), another series of paintings from Maisur in the South, more power-inflated, loads its vigorous design and hieratic figures with gold and stylistic ornaments of temple art (nos. 117-121). The school of Tanjore, in the South, infuses stereotyped Western naturalism into this blend, removing at times its staleness by the naïvité of preoccupations or superstitions which can be satisfied by just this type of art (no. 112).

In the field of sculpture, the polychrome wood carvings of Kerala on the southwest coast are more than equivalent to the Maisur paintings (nos. 127-134). Their epic chattiness derives from earlier, near Hoysala idioms; never before have hands been so weighty and fingers so elongated as in this carved and painted exuberance showing the hosts of gods, heroes and demons on temple beams and cars. Such reliefs are created in, and again help to create, a consistent mood of religious absorption. The spell of autochthony pervades them.[106]

On a corresponding level of autochthonous tradition, metal figurines from the Western Himalayas are far from consistent in their form. Daringly or clumsily they present long-lived dregs of classical Western art, reduced simulacra of Himalayan temple art and a pristine aptitude for turning iconography into newly discovered simplicities of form (nos. 202-209; plate xxxvi).

Steeped in the rites of their own living traditions of art which went on even when the Great Tradition of the temple builders was given no further scope, the craftsmen throughout India, from about the sixteenth century, supplied the needs of temple worship. Temple cars, in which the image of deity is taken in procession, continued to be built. Indian textbooks on architecture distinguish stationary from mobile architecture. The latter is preeminently that of the temple car. In the two last centuries, it remained a showplace for sacred imagery (nos. 98, 132-134), fulfilling in its own scale the purpose of the temple: to be seen. To have a look *(darshana)* of the temple, to see and to take in all that it stands for was the main purpose of a visit to a temple. All the meaning and power inherent in it comes out on its walls as sculpture. The centrifugal impact from the core and centre of the temple on to the walls and thence on the beholder generates a dynamism of sculptural form active even in the latest carvings of a wooden temple car, about a century ago (no. 98). Here, an age-old tradition is still a vital creative urge, manifest in the vehement massing of rhythms which overcome the somewhat stale shapes of the figures. It is by its driving power of rhythmic organization that Indian village art, where it stems from the Great Tradition, is not a folk art. It does not apply to its own scale a great heritage, but contributes to it.

The Indian image-maker of the Great Tradition complied with a detailed iconography and iconometry according to his own artistic endowment. The rules let him soar above their firm foundation or they tied him down. If he but followed the rules with sculptural competence, his work became fit for worship. When the Great Tradition no longer prevailed, the village craftsmen shaped images which were iconographically acceptable,[107] though their iconometry was no longer necessarily that of the canons of temple art. Distortions, formerly present but kept in check by these canons, had now a wider scope. In their inflexions, the rural, tribal idiosyncratic tendencies and heritage expressed themselves. God Krishna now plays his games or his flute—which is hardly ever represented in sculpture—in as many distinct modes as the rhythms of modelling and proportions of his body convey in his Rajasthani or Orissan or Bengali image (nos. 24, 284, 316, 326). If Hindu or Jain images are given form by the rural craftsman, they are shaped according to the rhythms of his own way of realizing their presence (nos. 46, 127, 160-162, 201; plates xx, xxi). On the other hand, and at the same time, he may follow the example of Hindu temple art (nos. 327, 328; plates xxvi, xxvii), and he may visualize the gods and ghosts who protect or threaten his village—instead of marking their presence by an unhewn stone—and invest their images with the substance of Hindu form (nos. 113-116). He models their figures so that they expand in planes rounded as if by the pulsations of life and breath which here do not come from their core. Something seems to hold back their luxuriant ease, something that links them to the sterner conceptions of tribal art. At other times, a truly aboriginal conception of a *rakshasa*, a man-eating ogre, seems almost to have invented its own technique, a slashed hollow cast whose ribbands streak the cylinders of the legs and furrow the "naturalism" of the head (no. 89; plate xxii), whereas an image of Navagunjara (no. 285; plate xix) is as much a product of local theology as it is an Indian representative of the "animal style" and a creation of the village art of Orissa. Ritual implements, such as ritual lamps (nos. 126, 251) and vessels (nos. 353, 354) and objects of domestic ritual, such as body scrubbers (no. 176), and also magic wands (no. 325; plate xlviii), are equally significant works of art. In extraordinary diversity, they emerge from below the cover of the once unifying Great Tradition.

In the domestic art of the *kantha,* the embroidered field had taken to its own use the magical disposition of the floor paintings *(alpona)*. The embroidered coverlets of the Western Himalayas,[108] though not magically strengthened by the art of stitching, were also made to be gifts (nos. 213-218). The drawing, however, was often done by professional artists whose work are the Pahari miniature paintings stemming from several stylistically distinct local centres (nos. 213, 214). The elegance of these embroideries of the higher social classes is set off by others, less ambitious in scale and narrative, where tribal phantasies are at play (no. 215). Between such extremes of conception, but worked in the same satin stitch with floss silk on gossamer thin handspun, handwoven cotton, in the colours of Pahari miniatures, are all-over designs of rustic simplicity and visual integrity (no. 217).

Textiles as covers, wall hangings, and colourful canopies offered their embroidered or appliquéd fields as decorations particularly at marriages (nos. 62, 72-78, 196) but also as a tribute to a dead saint or hero (no. 195; plate xl). The symbols and figures of these textiles accompany the ritual of the living and those for the dead in rural India.[109]

Part of the ritual are also the shadow plays with their painted figures. They are ancient means of religious instruction—an involuntary learning by seeing and listening—and entertainment.[110] The puppets, made of painted deer- or goatskin, are either semi-transparent, as in the "dance of the leather puppets" of Andhra-desha in the eastern Deccan (nos. 182-187; plate xxix) or, cut out of buffalo skin, they are opaque as are those of Kerala on the southwest coast (nos. 138-142), their heroic figures belong to the Ramayana. Seen on the screen, they are but shadows, projections of an exemplary reality. As such, their function is at the other end from that of the masks. The mask shields inner reality, the presence of the numinous, and the person possessed by it from the outer world, while at the same time impressing the outer world with the form of the numinous. Masks are tribal creations. They are essential means of identification with a superhuman reality by one who experiences this reality and, being the form created out of this experience, they are a means of communication between that reality and those who are in need of sensing its presence. The shadow play on the screen, on the other hand, and the painted scrolls, the embroideries and other kinds of rural art conjure up and trace images inwardly seen. They adumbrate and illustrate the other world so that it may find its place in this world and through its form in art enter the pattern of life.

The gap in intensity in tribal art on the one hand and rural art on the other is closed, in India, by the penetration of tribal into village art. This blend, by the nineteenth century, took to itself some of the shapes and finally also some of the flavour of Western naturalism such as the British patronized. It was this Western naturalism which took over where Indian "naturalism" of the Great Tradition of temple art had left off. Tribal art, although restricted and impoverished today, had given more to Hindu village art than it received in turn—and what tribal art did receive, it partly received it back. The charm of the equestrian figurines (nos. 25-34, 228; plates xi-xvi) seems to have been gathered in this way.

A figurine made by the village potter, or by a woman, if consecrated, plays its part in the rites. If not consecrated, it is a plaything. Toys made of clay, wood, cloth or pith (nos. 57, 58, 192, 295-297, 333-341, 355-356, 362, 447), simple in the stereometry of their shape, heightened by colour, are functional. While they delight sight and touch, they quicken the imagination. Other toys, more detailed in execution because representational in intent, incorporate their once ritual purpose in the ever stimulating qualities of the traditional materials of which they are made (nos. 357, 358). With this added grace, they are easy to look at, being of the same lineage as the figures in the embroideries and scroll paintings made in the village.

Notes

[1]Surajit Sinha, "Tribal Cultures of Peninsular India," *Traditional India,* ed. M. Singer (Philadelphia, 1959), pp. 298-311. The figures in the preceding paragraph refer to India proper, not to the entire subcontinent.

[2]G. N. Das, "The Funerary Monuments of the Nilgiris," *Bulletin of the Deccan College Research Institute,* XVIII (Poona, 1957), 140-152; James W. Breeks, *An Account of the Primitive Tribes and Monuments of the Nilgiris* (London, 1873), Pls. XXXVI-XXXIX.

[3]Verrier Elwin, *The Tribal Art of Middle India* (Oxford, 1951), p. 2. The statement by Panini (VI.2.62) classifies without evaluation. A distinction however, recorded in later days, though not aimed at the visual arts but at music, is relevant. The Sangita Darpana (I.4-6) contrasts *marga* with *deshi: marga* implies the path of sacred tradition, *deshi* a local or "country" style, the one safeguarding the purity of the tradition on the side of the performer and the knowledge of its subtleties on the side of the audience, the other being unconcerned with its rules. Applied to visual art, deviations from the established iconometry would make a work of art *deshi,* i.e. belonging to "folk art." This term does apply to the work of the rural *chitrakaras* of the later nineteenth and early twentieth century in Bengal whose scroll paintings illustrate Hindu themes. It does not apply to works of art outside the Hindu tradition, and in which content and form correspond the one to the other.

[4]*Indian Archaeology 1959-60—A Review* (New Delhi, 1960), p. 18, Pl. XVI; M. G. Dikshit, "Excavations at Rangpur, 1947," *Bulletin of the Deccan College Research Institute,* XI (Poona, 1950), 51, Pl. XVII.

[5]W. Koppers, "Die Bhil in Zentral Indien," *Wiener Beiträge zur Kulturgeschichte und Linguistik,* VII (Vienna, 1948), 17.

[6]Koppers, *op. cit.,* p. 20. C. von Fürer-Haimendorf, in T. B. Naik, *The Bhils* (Delhi, 1956), p. x.

[7]Mathias Hermanns, *Die Religiös-Magische Weltanschauung der Primitivstämme Indiens* (Wiesbaden, 1964), I, 13.

[8]Koppers, *op. cit.,* p. 14.

[9]Koppers, "Monuments to the Dead Erected by the Bhils and their Neighbours," *Annali Lateranensi,* VI (1942), 119-206, *passim.*

[10]Rig Veda, I. 163.2.

[11]*Agni Purana,* ch. 51, 3. Images of Surya, the sun-god, on horseback are in the great sun temples of Martand, Kashmir, of the eighth century and in Konarak, Orissa, of the thirteenth century. Cf. H. Goetz, "The Mediaeval Sculpture of Kashmir," *Marg,* VIII, 65f, Fig. 3; H. Zimmer, *The Art of Indian Asia* (New York, 1955), Pl. 371; M. Th. de Mallmann, *Les Enseignments Iconographiques de l'Agni Purana* (Paris, 1963), p. 76.

[12]Cf. Rig Veda, IV. 40. 5; VII. 77.3.

[13]Hermanns, *op. cit.,* pp. 403-426, treating of the Bhagoria Bhil, and Koppers, "Die Bhil . . ." pp. 207ff. The accounts differ in some respects according to variations of the Nukto rites in different localities within the Bhil region.

[14]Koppers, "Die Bhil . . ." pp. 147, 260.

[15]J. Abbot, *The Keys of Power* (London, 1932), p. 10.

[16]For example, see *1000 Years of Iranian Art,* Smithsonian Institution, exhibition catalogue, 1964-65, Fig. 104.

[17]Leonhard Adam, *Primitive Art* (London, 1954), Pl. 11b.

[18]The surface patterns of the wire-technique in metal recall those produced by the coiled withes of Siki grass of which figurines and baskets are made to this day in North Bihar. See Ruth Reeves, *Cire Perdue Casting in India* (New Delhi, 1962), p. 17, *passim.* In the equestrian figurines from Western India, the body of the horse is sometimes cast hollow.

[19]*Aitareya Brahmana,* III. 33.

[20]J. Dowson, *A Classical Dictionary of Hindu Mythology and Religion* (London, 1914), p. 311.

[21]Brahmanic texts know not only the skin but also the horn of the black antelope to be full of secret powers. Cf. H. Oldenburg, *Vorwissenschaftliche Wissenschaft: Die Weltanschauung der Brahmana Texte* (Göttingen, 1919), p. 42. During the Soma sacrifice, the priest wrapped a horn of the black antelope into his robe, saying "Thou art the maternal lap of Indra." The skin of a black antelope is the initiation garment of a Brahman (*Institutes of Vishnu* [Sacred Books of the East] VII, 115).

A black antelope skin is also the seat of a Brahman during meditation. An early Chola relief shows the antelope as Vahana of Durga, the Great Goddess (S. R. Balasubrahmanyam, *Early Chola Art* (Bombay, 1966), Pt. I, Pl. 1b.). Horse and deer are also known as the vehicles of the luminaries (Abbot, *op. cit.,* p. 142), the solar symbolism of the horse being pervasive. In the small metal images the shapes of deer and antelope are assimilated the one to the other.

[22]The "wire" technique is being practiced by itinerant or settled metal workers in West Bengal, South Bihar, Mayurbhanj, Orissa and in Madhya Pradesh as far south as Bastar. It is not always possible to assign on grounds of style alone each figurine to its place of origin. However, the Kaser of Bastar evolved a distinct style of the wire-technique. The figurines made for the Kutiya Kond tribe of Orissa are another style group by themselves. Other figurines from Orissa (no. 286) do not resemble them. The work of Ruth Reeves (note 18) devoted to the hereditary metal craftsmen working for tribal and non-tribal peoples in certain parts of Middle and Eastern India needs to be carried on wherever vestiges of traditional crafts survive.

[23]Hermanns, *op. cit.,* p. 499, Pl. XIII, Fig. 24. The wheel is a symbol of the sun (Rig Veda, IV.30.4). Sun wheels are imprinted on the palms and soles of the Buddha according to the verbal possible to assign on grounds of style alone each figurine to its place of origin. However, the Kaser fish (no. 245) are attributes of their nature as deities. Re. the sanctity of the wheel, cf. no. 417.

[24]A. J. Patel, "Folk Terra-cottas of Gujarat," *Journal of M. S. University of Baroda,* XII (1963), 63-67 discusses such "substitute" offerings donated in lieu of the actual animal. P. Jayakar, "Some Terra-cotta Figurines from Tribal Gujarat," *Marg,* VII (1953), 27-32, states that the terra-cotta figurines of the Rani Paraj areas of Surat are made by the potter women solely for the tribal people. The Rani Paraj terra-cottas have a fantastic, flamboyant style.

[25]Their number is not accidental, 72 being 9 times 8, the sacred number of the "city of Ayodhya," the "perfect dwelling" that is, the body of man. Cf. Stella Kramrisch, *The Hindu Temple* (Calcutta, 1946), I, 49.

[26]A. Chandras, "Gujarat Fairs and Festivals," *Census of India* (New Delhi, 1961), V, Pt. VII, B, 228.

[27]A. K. Coomaraswamy, *The Indian Craftsman* (London, 1909), p. 21.

[28]Louis Dumont, "Définition structurale d'un dieu populaire Tamoul: Aiyanar, Le Maître," *Journal Asiatique,* CCXLVI (1953), 256-270.

[29]Pyyappan, *Lord Ayyappan,* Bharatiya Vidya Bhavan (Bombay, 1962), p. 55.

[30]Dumont, *op. cit.,* p. 263.

[31]H. Whitehead, *The Village Gods of South India* (London, 1921), p. 26.

[32]*Folk Arts of India,* catalogue section by Ruth Reeves (Syracuse, 1967), pp. 33-34.

[33]Stirrups on horses are shown in Indian stone sculptures of ca. the first century B.C. to the first century A.D. in Sanchi, Bhaja, Pitalkhora and Mathura. S. D. Singh, *Ancient Indian Warfare with Special Reference to the Vedic Period* (Leiden, 1965), p. 63, asserts that this is the first occurrence in any representation not only in India, of stirrups, however primitive they are.

[34]W. G. Archer, *The Vertical Man, A Study in Primitive Sculpture* (London, 1947), p. 44.

[35]B. K. Sarkar, *The Folk Element in Hindu Culture* (London, 1917), p. 111.

[36]A. Bhattacharya, "The Cult of the Village Gods of West Bengal," *Man in India,* XXXV (1955), 19-33.

[37]Reeves, *Folk Arts . . .,* p. 33.

[38]Kramrisch, *op. cit.,* p. 32.

[39]Cf. note 37.

[40]The votive images of bullocks and horses in some of the South Indian village sanctuaries form large herds of animal statuary whose impact by sheer number of their repetitive shapes is as powerful as that of the human votive figures, offered for warding off epidemics (Pls. I, II). They form a dam of cumulative units against apprehensions and fears. Similarly, in Malabar, local ghosts, the servants of the goddess who could bring misfortune, must be offered bullocks and horses. E. K. Gough, "Cults of the Dead among the Nayars," *Traditional India,* ed. M. Singer (Philadelphia, 1959), p. 260.

[41]While Bhagavan, Supreme Deity, is without an image, the gods of Hinduism accepted into the tribal pantheon, as well as the lesser, originally tribal gods and also the tribalised versions of Hindu gods, have their images set up for worship, for instance by the Bhil (Ramesh Chand, "The Painted Terra-cotta Wall Plaques of Molela Village," *Folk Arts of India* [Syracuse, 1967], pp. 63-68). It must not be overlooked that some of the Hindu gods were of pre-Hindu or tribal origin. But it was within Hinduism that their iconic shapes were conceived.

[42]According to the information given by the Victoria and Albert Museum, London, the figurines are "playthings for the use of the bridegroom (generally about ten years old)."

[43]Elwin, *op. cit.,* pp. 173, 175, Fig. 196.

[44]Outside the work of Verrier Elwin, Ruth Reeves and W. G. Archer, no local studies have been made. Anthropological publications have given no further attention to tribal and rural art but that of bare reference to its existence and hardly any illustration.

The metal statuettes travel easily. When they finally reach a dealer, he mostly does not know their place of origin. They are summarily known as "Jungli bronzes."

[45]Elwin, *op. cit.,* p. 2.
The name of these metal smiths is variously spelt: Kaser, Ghadwa, or Ghasia. W. Grigson, *The Maria Gonds of Bastar* (Oxford, 1938), p. 179 spoke of them as "one of the lowest of the untouchable castes." "Even in Bastar where many of them are skilled artisans, the wildest Maria hold them in profound contempt." The untouchables, or "scheduled castes" or "God's people," (Harijan) as Gandhi called them, are mainly of tribal or "aboriginal" stock. Outcast and despised, they remained creative and kept their craft traditions intact.

[46]Elwin, *op. cit.,* Figs. 136, 138, 140, 141; the carvings by the Hill Saora of Ganjam, Orissa, representing Sahibosum.

[47]James Tod, *Annals and Antiquities of Rajasthan,* ed. C. W. Crooke (London, 1908), I, 262.

[48]A large group of figures from the temple at Darasuram, carved in stone and representing "The Wives of the Rishis" (now in the Tanjore Art Gallery) is an exception. *The Tanjore Art Gallery Guide Book* (Tanjore, 1957), p. xxvii.

[49]S. C. Roy, *The Oraons of Chota Nagpur* (Ranchi, 1915), p. 185.

[50]The masks, collected by V. Elwin and now in the collection of the National Museum, New Delhi, are all too few. They do not allow generalizations on behalf of their form with reference to the tribe which made them.

[51]Sarkar, *op. cit.,* p. 110.

[52]Cf. Balwant Gargi, *Folk Theater of India* (Washington, 1966), pp. 166-181.

[53]A. K. Coomaraswamy, *History of Indian and Indonesian Art,* 1966, p. 108, Pl. XCI, Fig. 273. King Hemaprakasha was the donor of this mask from Nirmand.

[54]From Buddhist monuments of the later part of the first millennium B.C. (with their golden plaques of the Earth-goddess) and possibly from the Vedic age with its effigy of the "golden man."

[55]On the East gate of Sanchi (first century B.C. to first century A.D.). J. Marshall and A. Foucher, *The Monuments of Sanchi,* Vol. II, Pl. 49a. On the door jambs of the Dashavatar Temple at Deogarh (early sixth century), Stella Kramrisch, *The Art of India* (London, 1965), Pl. 48.

[56]Grigson, *op. cit.,* p. 281; Elwin, *op. cit.,* p. 71.

[57]The horseman, however, as Spirit Rider, whose past extends from Hindu and Aryan to pre-Aryan times is not only the ancestral symbol of the Bhil, where it is cast in metal and carved in stone, but also of the Korku of Middle India (Elwin, *op. cit.,* p. 90), whose wooden memorial posts show the figure of the ancestral Spirit Rider with the sun and moon, the ultimate ancestors, above.

[58]Dakshinaranjan Shastri, "Cult and Images of Pitris," *Journal of the Indian Society of Oriental Art,* VII (1939), 72-73.

Ancestral effigy and sacrifice post (to which in Vedic rites, the animal was fastened before being immolated) are amalgamated here. In Hindu thought, the bull is a symbol of righteousness and cosmic law, or *dharma,* (*Vishnudharmottara Purana* [Baroda, 1958] III, 48.18).

[59]Cf. The hobbyhorse of the Durjat Shamans, in W. Koppers, "Pferdeopfer und Pferdekult der Indogermanen," *Wiener Beiträge zur Kulturgeschichte und Linguistik,* IV (1936), 374. The hobbyhorse of the Muria and Maria Gond is the subject of an article by V. Elwin on "The Hobby Horse," *Illustrated Weekly of India* (Bombay, July 5, 1953). Cf. Sarkar, *op. cit.,* p. 111, and Stephen Fuchs, *The Gond and Bhumia of Eastern Mandla* (New York, 1959), p. 448.

[60]Control of the senses is also enjoined for the Hindu craftsman. (*Shilparatna,* I. 2ff.)

[61]C. von Fürer-Haimendorf, *Naked Nagas* (Calcutta, 1962), p. 52.

[62]V. Elwin, *The Art of the North-East Frontier of India* (Shillong, 1959), p. 5.

[63]Similar in shape to the *mukh-dibba,* the face-casket used in Bengal for serving "pan" (nos. 323, 324).

[64]When erecting a new building, the sacrifice of a human being strengthened the new building. This belief is widespread in India, too, and seems to underlie the myth of the Vastupurusha.

[65]This aristocrat (he was alive in 1962) was—or is—a blacksmith; his brothers are wood carvers. C. von Fürer-Haimendorf (*op. cit.,* p. 114), says that "the only things he was really serious about were his works of art."

[66]A comparison with wooden Muria figures from Middle India (no. 152) of about the same degree of tribal form shows the "elegance" of this Naga style.

[67]Elwin, *The Tribal Art . . . ,* p. 173.

[68]Cf. Pictures painted on the wall of their houses by the Saora following the inspiration of a dream. *Ibid.* Figs. 209-216, 222.

[69]*Shilparatna,* chap. 46. 143-145.

[70]By Oraon, Munda, Kharia and Birhor; cf. S. C. Roy, *Oraon Religion and Customs* (Ranchi, 1928), pp. 285f. The drawing on the ground of an enclosure (square or circular) and quartered is common to the Bhil, Baiga, etc., as it is with the Hindus; cf. Fuchs, *op. cit.,* pp. 267, 452.

[71]C. W. Crooke, *The Popular Religion and Folklore of Northern India* (London, 1896), II, 191.

[72]Tantric religion gives prominence to the female principle in divinity and to the union with it. Tantric ritual uses complex diagrams as symbolic and magical contrivances *(yantra)* in and by which deity is beheld in its cosmic manifestation and primordial unity.

[73]Cf. G. Tucci, *The Theory and Practice of the Mandala* (London, 1961), pp. 49-84.

[74]Abbot, *op. cit.,* p. 14.

[75]They are strictly geometrical in Western and South India and are called *mandana* in Rajasthan, *rangoli* in Maharashtra, *sathiya* in Gujarat, and *kolam* (and *muggu*) in South India. They are richer in symbolic shapes in Bengal, Bihar and elsewhere in Northern India where they are

known as *alpona* and *aripana; apna* is their name in the Western Himalaya, *cowka purna* and *sona rakhna* in Uttar Pradesh. The *paglya* of Rajasthan include footprints in their designs as do certain *alpona.*

Cf. W. T. Elmore, *Dravidian Gods in Modern Hinduism* (University of Nebraska Studies, 1915), p. 27, Pl. IV; J. Layard, "Labyrinth Ritual in South India," *Folklore,* LXIII-LXIV (1952-53) 463-472.

[76]T. M. Chatterji, *Alpona* (Calcutta, 1948), No. 32, p. 58. Also, S. K. Ray, *The Ritual Art of the Bratas of Bengal* (Calcutta, 1961), pp. 41-48.

[77]C. G. Diehl, *Instrument and Purpose* (Lund, 1956), p. 252, re: the encircling of power; Abbot, *op. cit.,* p. 83; re: the function of the ground.

[78]*Vishnudharmottara Purana,* Pt. II, chap. 169. The text is of the sixth century but goes back to older sources. The "lotus flower" here is a symbol, a *rose des vents,* pointing into the eight directions. An actual lotus flower has petals in multiples of five.

[79]Puranas are encyclopaedias of traditional knowledge, dealing with everything from the creation of the cosmos onwards.

[80]*Brahma, P.,* 28. 23-33; *Bhavishya P.,* 48.52,205. *Shamba P.,* 29. 2-6, saying that the sun was worshipped in a circle by his devotees "in early days," that is prior to the anthropomorphic image of the sun-god. This is shown on coins dating from ca. 200 B.C. to the first century A.D. (J. N. Banerjea, *The Development of Hindu Iconography* [Calcutta, 1956], pp. 138-139, Pl. II, 8.). Here the circular sun symbol is raised on an altar.

[81]Haradatta commenting on Gautama Sutra 11.20 says that when the sun stands in Aries young girls paint the sun and his retinue on the soil with coloured dust and worship this in the morning and in the evening. This is to illustrate the meaning of the Sutra which enjoins that customs though not expressly founded upon a passage of the Veda are to be observed if they are not against the principles of the sacred writings. Max Muller, *History of Ancient Sanskrit Literature* (London, 1859), p. 53. That the sacred symbol was drawn on the ground was a non-Vedic practice.

All the same, the Vedic altars range in plan from circle and square to complex geometrical configurations such as the shape of a bird. The laying of the bricks in these patterns would presuppose their being drawn on the ground.

[82]Stella Kramrisch, "Kantha," *Journal of the Indian Society of Oriental Art,* VII (Calcutta, 1939), 141-167; Kramrisch, "Kanthas of Bengal," *Marg,* III (1949), 18-29.

[83]Rig Veda 6.9.3; 10.130.1, also *Brihadaranyaka Upanishad,* III, 8.3-8 and *Mundaka Upanishad,* II.2.5.

[84]M. Lalou, *Iconographie des étoffes peintes (pata) dans le Manjusrimulakalpa* (Paris, 1930), p. 27.

[85]Crooke, *op. cit.,* p. 161.

[86]Sarkar, *op. cit.,* p. 33.

[87]Cf. K. K. Ganguli, "Kantha, The Enchanted Wrap," *Indian Folklore,* I, No. 2, 3-10.

[88]Kanthas, however, made by women of the weaver caste, imitate the effect of weaving and are meant to be seen on one side only. G. S. Dutt, "The Art of Kantha," *Modern Review* (Calcutta, October, 1939).

[89]J. C. Mathur, "Domestic Arts of Mithila," *Marg,* XX (1966), 43-46.

[90]W. G. Archer, "Maithil Painting," *Marg,* III (1949), 24-33.
Mildred Archer, "Notes on [Maithil] Paintings," *Marg,* XX (1966), 47.

[91]Crooke, *op. cit.,* p 28.

[92]Pran Nath Mago, "Murals and Mosaics from Villages around Delhi," *Design* (New Delhi, August, 1967), pp. 22-25. The peacock, bird of immortality, is painted on funerary urns of Harappa, cemetery II, of the second millennium B.C. In the rites of Sanjhi, the figures not only have their place on the wall, but also their specific time when they come to exist visually, in scale with the dimensions of the wall. If taken out of its ritual context, "the skilled work of those who practice folk art as a commercial craft" immediately degenerates into inane "decoration." Cf. *Design,* p. 30, showing a "village mural made by village women near Delhi for the Indian pavilion at Expo 67."

[93]A. K. Coomaraswamy, "Picture Showmen," *Indian Historical Quarterly,* V (1929), 182-184.

[94]S. K. Ray, "The Artisan Castes of West Bengal and Their Craft," *Census of India* (West Bengal, 1951), pp. 293-349.

[95]Stella Kramrisch, *The Hindu Temple,* p. 9, quoting *Brahmavaivarta Purana,* I. 10.20-23f.

[96]G. S. Dutt, "Tiger's God in Bengal Art," *Modern Review,* LII (1932), 521-529; G. S. Dutt,

"The Living Tradition of Folk Arts in Bengal," *Indian Art and Letters,* N. S. X (London, 1936), 34; G. S. Dutt, "The Indigenous Painters of Bengal," *Journal of the Indian Society of Oriental Art* (1932), p. 21. Contrary to G. S. Dutt, "Tiger's God . . ." W. G. Archer considers the "portraits" the work of *chitrakaras* and not of *jadu-patuas* (in a note to the writer).

[97] S. K. Ray, *op. cit.,* p. 311.

[98] A. Ghose, "Old Bengal Paintings," *Rupam* (Calcutta, 1926), pp. 27-28, Pls. 2 and 3, was unable at that time to assign these paintings to Hooghly or to Bankura.
Cf. A. Mookerjee, *Folk Art of Bengal* (Calcutta, 1946), Pl. XXI.

[99] D. P. Ghosh, "An Illustrated Ramayana Manuscript and Patas from Bengal," *Journal of the Indian Society of Oriental Art,* XIII (Calcutta, 1945), 134f.

[100] Coomaraswamy, *op. cit.,* note 92, referring to the Mudrarakshasa of the seventh to eighth century.

[101] Practically all the paintings come from West Bengal. However, the style of the Ghazi-pats in East Bengal is closely related to work of the *jadu-patuas* in the Santal Parganas of West Bengal and Bihar.

[102] C. Dev, "An Outline of the Folk Art of Bengal," *Indian Folklore,* II (Calcutta, 1959), 203.

[103] W. G. Archer, *Bazaar Paintings of Calcutta* (London, 1953). In W. G. Archer, *Kalighat Drawings* (Bombay, 1962), this term, however, is no longer used.

[104] Binayak Mishra, "Folklore and Pauranic Tradition about the Origin of God Jagannatha," *Indian Historical Quarterly,* XIII (1937), 600-609. The shape of a log of wood—which is that of the image of Jagannatha worshipped in the temple at Puri, Orissa on the east coast of India—serves also the tribal Muria and Maria Gond of Mid-India as nucleus of their log symbol called *pen* (Grigson, *op. cit.,* p. 194) and it underlies the shape of the goddess Kali as painted by the *patuas* of Kalighat, Bengal.

[105] Tod, *op. cit.,* I, 329; II, 893.

[106] Stella Kramrisch, *Dravida and Kerala* (Ascona, 1963), Pls. 33-37.

[107] Most of the stone images of this phase, while fit for the purpose of worship, are outside the realm of art.

[108] K. K. Ganguli, "Chamba Rumal," *Journal of the Indian Society of Oriental Art,* XI (Calcutta, 1943), Pl. facing p. 70.

[109] Shown in the present exhibition are only a few varieties of textiles of rural character which are more closely connected with the celebration of rites.

[110] Wooden puppets moved by strings were known at the time of the Mahabharata (3.30.21f) where the actions of men are compared to those of wooden puppets moved by strings, controlled by a power beyond them. Puppet plays, one of the oldest forms of the theatre in India, have a large audience to this day in Rajasthan. Their themes, however, belong to a large extent to the life of the court. Cf. A. K. Coomaraswamy " 'Spiritual Paternity' and the 'Puppet Complex,' " *Psychiatry,* VIII (1945), No. 3, 287.

Director's Note

The material of this exhibition has been created by successive generations of simple people as a response to their spiritual needs. It is an art of the transitory—repeatedly created for the particular moment to express, nonetheless, an eternal necessity. The very fact that these objects are so strongly traditional in their forms—whether they date from the third millennium B.C. or our own day—is a forceful indication of how deeply constant are the feelings that inspired them. These works stem from an unknown India whose rude strength is in such great contrast to the sophisticated traditions generally associated with the religious art of the Brahmanic tradition. Western eyes will find it an art that is a fascinating combination of naïveté and sensitive perception.

While the motivation is entirely different, certain of these works may easily remind the viewer of ones created by the artists of today. The images repeatedly suggest comparison with contemporary artists who have been deeply influenced by the art of children. Some of these compositions, by drawing upon the most common materials of their creators' villages, recall the art of the assemblage which has reached such heights in our time. The attitudes behind the handling of the techniques of the *kantha* textiles, in which the development of the minute but sprawling brightly-colored patterns are dictated by the weaknesses of the fabric, are thoroughly sympathetic to the automatism of the early surrealists. Yet in the hands of the succeeding generations of Indian artists each of these techniques is significantly interrelated with the basic spiritual meaning behind the creation of the object, usually a meaning related to the transformation of the insignificant. That this material is so little known in the West is perhaps explained by the fact that not before today has there been an atmosphere which would properly accept some of the methods and attitudes which created it.

The excitement of the exhibition—as well as its difficulty—has stemmed from the material which has never been generally studied with such method. Dr. Stella Kramrisch, the Philadelphia Museum of Art's Curator of Indian Art, has after years of study in India, attempted to coordinate the many aspects of ritual art—tribal and rural—of the Indian subcontinent. In terms of this exhibition India is, of course, intended to mean the subcontinent of India; certain of the areas presented here are part of Pakistan. Also, while certain aspects of the ritual art of rural or tribal origin could not be included, every effort has been made to convey here the variety of treatment and attitude characteristic of the many traditions.

International exhibitions such as this require cooperation on many levels. The three exhibiting museums are certainly aware that without the help given by Mrs. Indira Gandhi, Prime Minister of India, the exhibition could never have been realized, and we are, therefore, most deeply grateful. Mr. M. C. Chagla, formerly the Minister of Education of the Government of India, has been unstinting in his keen interest in the basic subject matter of the exhibition; His Excellency, B. K. Nehru, Ambassador of India in Washington, and Mrs. B. K. Nehru have been extraordinarily generous in their unfailing intervention to assure the exhibition's materializing; thanks are also due to Kamala Devi Chattopadhyaya and to Dr. Grace Morley, Advisor on Museums, New Delhi and formerly Director of the San Francisco Museum of Art, for their generosity and ever-ready advice. Two grants from the JDR 3rd Fund have significantly assisted in the financing of the exhibition; the first made it possible for Dr. Kramrisch to personally negotiate in India the loans so lavishly granted by several museums and private collectors while the second enabled the Indian Curator accompanying the exhibition, Mr. Haku Shah, to travel in the United States. We must also thank Dr. Kapila Vatsyayan and Mr. T. S. Swaminathan of the Ministry of Education, Government of India, for their patient efficiency in seeing matters through, as well as Mr. W. G. Archer, Dr. Moti Chandra, Mr. Devaprasad Ghosh, Dr. Anand Krishna, Mr. Pran Nath Mago, and Mr. Sudhansu Kumar Ray for their valuable information.

Mr. Harry Holtzman has been most cooperative in letting us use his photographic material which splendidly communicates the message of the materials of this exhibition in an original setting.

Our great debt of thanks must go to the lenders. The material is to be exhibited for a considerable period of time; thus their cooperation is particularly appreciated. The broader discovery of art forms which has given the lenders such pleasure should add welcome dimensions to our knowledge of a still little known India.

Evan H. Turner
Director
Philadelphia Museum of Art

Lenders

Anonymous
Archaeological Museum, Mathura, Uttar Pradesh
Mildred and W. G. Archer Collection
Asutosh Museum of Indian Art, University of Calcutta
Poonam Backliwal, New Delhi
Gurusaday Museum—Bengal Bratachari Society
C. L. Bharany, New Delhi
Bion A. Bowman, Boston, Massachusetts
British Museum, London
Pamela Bull, Villanova, Pennsylvania
Vittorio Cacciandra, Bombay (and Milan)
Pramod Chandra, Chicago
Crafts Museum, New Delhi
Nirubhai Desai, Ahmedabad
Mr. and Mrs. Thomas C. Dove
Mrs. J. L. Eastwick, Charlestown, Pennsylvania
Fogg Art Museum, Cambridge, Massachusetts
Arts and Crafts Museum, Gandhi Smriti, Bhavnagar (Gujarat)
Collection of Mr. and Mrs. James Greene
D. P. Ghosh, Calcutta
Government Museum, Madras
Harry Holtzman, Lyme, Connecticut
Mrs. Pupul Jayakar, New Delhi
Clifford R. Jones, Rochester, New York
J. J. Klejman, New York
Craig Makler, Philadelphia
Collection: Master Benjamin Marks, New York
The Metropolitan Museum of Art, New York
Mr. and Mrs. Earl Morse, New York
Manu Narang, Bombay
National Museum, New Delhi
Collection, Dorothy Norman, New York
Philadelphia Museum of Art, Philadelphia
Courtesy Trustees of the Prince of Wales Museum of Western India, Bombay
Dr. O. W. Samson, London
Haku Shah, Ahmedabad
Robert M. Shapazian, Fresno, California
Nalini and Haridas K. Swali
Mrs. Srimati Tagore, Calcutta
Jennifer Turner, Philadelphia
John Turner, Philadelphia
Mrs. Aruna Vasudev, New Delhi
Victoria and Albert Museum, London
William H. Wolff, New York

Unknown India:
Ritual Art in Tribe and Village

*To be shown in Philadelphia only.

I Terra-cotta and Clay Figurines,
3rd Millennium B.C. to 20th Century A.D.
(nos. 1-22)

1 Humped Bull
Plate IX
Mohenjo-Daro, West Pakistan
Terra-cotta; 2⅝″ x 2″ x 1¼″
Later part 3rd millennium B.C.
National Museum, New Delhi
#DK 3651/241

Hand modelled, parts affixed and holed.

2 Figurine with Hat
Mohenjo-Daro, West Pakistan
Terra-cotta; 5½″ x 2″ x 1¼″
Later part 3rd millennium B.C.
Published: *Kunst aus Indien* (Zurich:
1960), Plate 1.
National Museum, New Delhi
#HR 5368/255

The nude figurine may be that of a
hermaphrodite. It wears a triple necklace
with pendents and a tall hatlike headdress.
Large, hollowed navel. Traces of painted
stripes on arms and a triangular band
from shoulders to chest. Modelled with
parts affixed.

3 Female Figurine
Mathura, Uttar Pradesh
Grey terra-cotta; 3″ x 1¾″ x 1¼″
ca. 6th century B.C.
Anonymous

Hand modelled, face pinched. Long eyes
incised, ringlets incised all over the long,
broad neck and body. Flat back.
Broken at wrist, arms missing.

4 Female Figurine
Mathura, Uttar Pradesh
Grey terra-cotta; 8⅞″ x 4¾″
ca. 3rd century B.C.
Archaeological Museum, Mathura, Uttar
Pradesh #40.2904.6

Hand modelled with ornaments affixed.
Face moulded. The flat abdominal part with
broad hips forming a segment of a circle
contrasts with the otherwise volumetric
shape of the figurine. The pelvic width
indicates that this figurine is of the class
of mother-goddesses.

5 Ram
Patna, Bihar
Terra-cotta; 3¼″ x 3¼″ x 1⅛″
2nd-1st century B.C.
Anonymous

Circles and lines incised on head and chest.

6 Horse
Patna, Bihar
Terra-cotta; 2½″ x 2⅛″ x ¹⁵⁄₁₆″
2nd-1st century B.C.
Anonymous

Small circles and short parallel lines
incised on back.

7 Horse
Patna, Bihar
Terra-cotta; 2⁹⁄₁₆″ x 3⅜″ x 1¼″
2nd-1st century B.C.
Anonymous

With lines incised on mane, circular and
straight lines on back.

8 Female Figurine
Taxila, West Pakistan
Terra-cotta; h: 4½″
1st century B.C. to 2nd century A.D.
Published: *The Art of India* (The Asia
Society, New York: 1962), Plate 3.
Fogg Art Museum, Cambridge, Massachusetts
#1937.25.12

9 Female Figurine
Sari Dheri, West Pakistan
Terra-cotta; h: 3½″
1st century B.C. to 2nd century A.D.
Published: *The Art of India* (The Asia
Society, New York: 1962), Plate 4.
Fogg Art Museum, Cambridge, Massachusetts
#1937.25.8

Flat figurine, vase shaped from hips
downward, short conical arm stumps.

10 Horse
Sari Dheri, West Pakistan
Terra-cotta; h: 4⅜″
1st-3rd century A.D.
Published: *The Art of India* (The Asia
Society, New York: 1962), Plate 5.
Fogg Art Museum, Cambridge, Massachusetts
#1937.25.11

11 Humped Bull
Sari Dheri, West Pakistan
Terra-cotta; 4½″ x 5½″
ca. 2nd century A.D.
Victoria and Albert Museum, London
#I.S.23-1961

12 Humped Bull
Sari Dheri, West Pakistan
Terra-cotta; 4″ x 4¾″
ca. 2nd century A.D.
Victoria and Albert Museum, London
#I.M.163-1937

The combination of basic shape and realistic
modelling is found in a class of popular
figurines which are made to this day.

13 Serpent Figurine
Patna, Bihar
Terra-cotta; 4¾″ x 2⅜″ x ¹⁵⁄₁₆″
ca. 2nd-3rd century A.D.
Anonymous

With large rings incised on significant parts
corresponding to breasts, navel, thighs;
flat, wide hip portion streaked with
incised long diagonal lines and short
intermittent lines in the opposite direction.

14 Seated Figurine
Maholi, Mathura, Uttar Pradesh
Terra-cotta; 8⅔″ x 3″
1st-3rd century A.D.
Archaeological Museum, Mathura,
Uttar Pradesh #64.7.6

Seated with legs pendent on a stool.
Three children (now mostly broken)
clinging to the large-headed, bejewelled
figure modelled crudely and vivaciously,
with naturalistic intent.

*15 Lid of Funerary Urn
Nilgiris, South India
Terra-cotta; 9¾″ x 6″
ca. 1st century A.D.
British Museum, London #11

The high neck of the circular convex lid
serves as a stool for an elongated female
figure whose pendent, cylindrical legs
and flattened body are surmounted by a
sturdy, flat neck of excessive length with a
small, concave, raised face. The figure
wears a "miniskirt" impressed with rows
of dots and lines, crossing neck ornament
or scarf ending above the small (damaged)
breasts and a double choker necklace.
Arms broken, left hand resting on hip.

*16 Lid of Funerary Urn
Nilgiris, South India
Terra-cotta; 10½″ x 6¼″
ca. 1st century A.D.
British Museum, London #79.12-1.28

Standing, boldly abstract female figurine
on top of convex lid. Planar long body and
upper arms, small breasts, large navel
(as in no. 15), very short, heavy cylinders of
legs ending in long toes, incised, like the
"miniskirt," with parallel verticals. Upturned
concave, hexagonal face, large circular
incised eyes with inscribed hexagons, long
cylinder of arm raised from elbow with
hand holding vessel carried on the head.

*17 Male; Tomb Figurine
Nilgiris, South India
Terra-cotta; h: 6½″
ca. 1st century A.D.
British Museum, London #79.12-1.42

Upper part of long flat body only.
Bearded face with modelled large ringlets
indicating hair; arms broken.

*18 Buffalo; Tomb Figurine
Nilgiris, South India
Terra-cotta; 5½″ x 9″
ca. 1st century A.D.
British Museum, London #1

Ponderous volumes, incised, streaked
and holed.

*19 Long-Necked Bird; Tomb Figurine
Nilgiris, South India
Terra-cotta; h: 4″
ca. 1st century A.D.
British Museum, London #79.12-1.96

Sensitively distorted, volumetric shapes,
flared cylindrical stand instead of legs. Two,
not quite parallel lines incised on body create
an illusion of movement. Neck detachable.

*20 "Two-Necks"; Tomb Figurine
Nilgiris, South India
Terra-cotta; h: 5½″
ca. 1st century A.D.
British Museum, London #34

Forked volumetric shape of two sturdy
overlong necks coalescing in short, flared,
cylindrical stand impressed with dots.
The neck prongs are terminated by horizontal
heads shown as if breathing from open,
naturalistically modelled muzzles. The
stretching or shrinking of one or the other
body part, flattening and distension of
the upper arms, and concave faces on the
one hand are combined with a naturalistic
modelling of one or the other facial
feature on the other hand in the Nilgiri
terra-cottas. *Indische Kunst,* Catalogue of
exhibition held at Stuttgart (Württem-
bergischer Kunstverein: 1966), #1-12,
Fig. 6, assigns the terra-cottas to 500-250 B.C.

21 Humped Bull
Sirpur, Madhya Pradesh
Terra-cotta; 5¼″ x 5½″ x 2¾″
20th century
Asutosh Museum of Indian Art, University
of Calcutta #F.654

22 Mother and Child
Madaripur, Faridpur, East Bengal
(East Pakistan)
Sunbaked clay; 3″ x 3″
20th century
Published: M. K. Pal, *Catalogue of Folk
Art in the Asutosh Museum* (Calcutta: 1962),
pp. 9-10, Plate III.
Asutosh Museum of Indian Art, University
of Calcutta #T.584

Figurines of this kind are worshipped
by young girls in ritual performance of
vowed observances (kumari vrata).

II Western India (nos. 23-81)

A. Rajasthan (nos. 23-45)

23 Dipa-Lakshmi
Rajasthan
Brass; 8″ x 3″ x 2½″
17th-18th century
Anonymous

Lamp bearer. Squared shoulders; squat,
static masses disposed in cubic space; notched
edges of shirt and coiffure. Lamp missing.

21
—
22

24
—
35.

24 Krishna, Flute-Playing
Rajasthan
Brass; 5⅜″ x 2½″ x 1½″
ca. 18th century
Anonymous

The body, delicate with vestigial modelling, stands straight on both legs, the tubular arms bent like wires, the face with enormous eyes and straight peaked nose.

25 Equestrian Figurine
Plate XII
Rajasthan
Brass; 4¾″ x 5″ x 1″
16th-17th century
Anonymous

More solidly conceived in the round than nos. 26-30, figurines of this type discharge tensions in the curves of reins, halters, etc. The rider carries his shield strapped to his back and wears a "crown" with a knob. None of the equestrian figurines wields bow or arrow. None of the metal figurines of horses and riders is dated. Comparisons with dated and inscribed stone reliefs of equestrian figures from Rajasthan of the late 15th and 16th centuries (H. Goetz, *The Art and Architecture of Bikaner State* [Oxford: 1950], Plate 148) and with hero stones of ca. the 18th century from Gujarat (such as shown on Photograph 844/61 of the Director General of Archaeology in India; from Wadhwan) do not allow definite conclusions. (Cf. a brass horse, *Handbook of the Collections of the Baroda Museum and Picture Gallery* [Baroda: 1952], Plate LV, which is dated by H. Goetz into the 14th century, apparently on account of the shape of the brass chariot.)

26 Equestrian Figurine
Plate XIII
Rajasthan
Brass; 4¾″ x 3¾″ x 1⅛″
17th century
Anonymous

The curved legs of the slender horse, high curved neck and long muzzle, and the flat, umbrella-like hat perched on the high and thin cone of the crown of the rider are characteristic of one type of Spirit Rider from Rajasthan.

27 Equestrian Figurine
Plate XI
Rajasthan
Brass; 5⅛″ x 3½″ x 1 9/16″
17th century
Anonymous

"Archaic" face of horseman; forehead and nose forming one high ridge with eyes "affixed" similar to treatment of clay figurines. Very high-legged horse; shield and sword attached to side of rider.

28 Equestrian Figurine
Rajasthan
Brass; 4⅜″ x 3½″ x 1⅜″
17th century
Anonymous

29 Equestrian Figurine
Rajasthan
Brass; 4″ x 3″ x 1½″
17th century
Mr. and Mrs. Earl Morse, New York City

Flat-faced type of rider.

30 Equestrian Figurine
Rajasthan
Brass; 4″ x 2¾″ x 1¼″
17th century
Mr. and Mrs. Earl Morse, New York City

Flat-faced type of rider.

31 Equestrian Figurine
Plate XVI
Rajasthan
Brass; 3⅜″ x 3⅛″ x 1⅜″
18th century
Anonymous

Sturdy, inflated, basic shape of horse, accentuated and set off by tuft of mane and tail; very small rider figurine.

32 Equestrian Figurine
Rajasthan
Brass; 4″ x 4″ x 1½″
18th century
John Turner, Philadelphia

33 Equestrian Figurine
Rajasthan
Brass; 3″ x 3½″ x 7½″
18th century
Jennifer Turner, Philadelphia

34 Equestrian Figurine
Plate XIV
Rajasthan
Brass; 4¾″ x 4⅛″ x 1¼″
18th century
Anonymous

Less stylized; shield strapped to back of rider.

35 Sati Memorial Stone
Border of Rajasthan and Gujarat (Idar?)
Stone; 1′8¼″ x 6¾″
ca. 18th century
Vittorio Cacciandra, Bombay

Gabled slab suggestive of a marriage tent and showing figure of the dead warrior holding his sword in his right hand, his left resting on the shoulder of his faithful wife (Sati) who immolated herself when he had fallen. She stands on a pedestal, raising her right hand. The gesture is repeated by the large arm which issues from a memorial pillar to the right of the warrior. A Shiva-linga in the upper compartment shows that the Sati and the hero were devotees of Shiva. Sun and moon on right and left.

37
41 detail

36 Sati Memorial Stone
Border of Rajasthan and Gujarat (Idar?)
Stone; 1'7½" x 6¼"
ca. 18th century
Vittorio Cacciandra, Bombay

37 Offering Casket
Rajasthan
Wood, painted and varnished; 1'8" x 10½"
20th century
Crafts Museum, New Delhi #M/7/2490

The lid of the peacock-shaped casket
carries two small figures. Presented by a
girl as a gift of love to her brother,
at the annual Phuli celebration.

38 Toilet Scene (Toy)
Bansi, Rajasthan
Wood, painted and varnished; 5⅗" x 4⅕"
20th century
Crafts Museum, New Delhi #M/19/14

39 A, B Two White Rag Horses
Rajasthan
Rags and wood; 2'1½" x 1'1¾" x 6";
2'2" x 1'5" x 7", respectively
20th century
A Haku Shah, Ahmedabad
B Philadelphia Museum of Art,
Philadelphia #67-197-5

Offerings to Ram Devji, king of Rajasthan.
Kings were regarded as divine, particularly
as the Rama avatar of Vishnu.

40 Shalibhadra Charitra
Bikaner
Gouache painting on cloth; 2'1" x 8"
Late 18th century
Anonymous

The popular Jain story of Shalibhadra
is illustrated by a celestial chariot, carried
by elephants floating in the air, Shalibhadra
being attended by celestial nymphs.
In the lower, small panels of the painting
Shalibhadra is seen dallying with girls.
Re. the story of Shalibhadra, cf.
M. Bloomfield, "Salibhadra Caritra,"
Journal of the American Oriental Society,
XLIII (1923), 259.

41 "Pabuji-ki-Phard"
Mewar, Rajasthan
Gouache painting on cloth; 4'5" x 16'10"
ca. 1870
Anonymous

The noble hero Pabuji Rathore lived and
died, 25 years old, in the 14th century.
The beautiful Deval Devi rode on a splendid
black mare while tending her cattle in
the desert of Marwar. Deval was considered
an incarnation of Shakti (the Great Goddess).
Jind Raj, a baron of Jayal, saw and
coveted the splendid black mare Kesar
Kalimi, but Deval would part from her only
at the price of his head. Deval, fearing
for her safety after this incident, moved to the
land of the chief of Kohlugarh who treated

her like his own daughter. Deval gave her
black mare to Pabuji, his son, for they
esteemed each other greatly, and he promised
to protect her and her cattle at the cost
of his life. But a beautiful princess fell in
love with Pabuji on his beautiful mare, and
wanted Pabuji to marry her. He told her,
however, that he had pledged his life to see to
Deval's safety and that of her cattle.
Jind Raj in the meanwhile took away
Deval's cattle. In the form of a bird, Deval
informed Pabuji, and he left his bride during
the wedding rites, to keep his word. With
seven men he rode on Kalimi, the black
mare, against Jind Raj and his thousand
soldiers and rescued the cattle. But he was
mortally wounded and died, together
with the black mare. His bride immolated
herself as Sati and joined Pabuji in heaven.

Bards travel from place to place, set up
the painting in the open, and, singing and
dancing, narrate the story during one
full night. The main figures in the painting
are Pabuji with his four ministers and
the black mare. Parallel episodes from deeds
of the gods are incorporated in the painting.
The painting (phard), whose entire length
is 30 feet, is set up in the open. In front of
it a bard (Bhopa) recites, dances
and mimes the story.

42 Hanuman Saluting Rama
Mewar
Painting on paper; 8" x 10"
18th century
C. L. Bharany, New Delhi

43 Puppets
Jaipur, Rajasthan
Wood, carved and painted, and cloth;
height ranging from 1'2" to 1'9"
20th century
Crafts Museum, New Delhi #M/7/2127

Representing different characters, such
as Kaikeyi, Bharata, Sumitra, court guards,
court dancers, a deer, etc., from different
plots ranging from the Ramayana and
included in the tragic puppet play of
Rao Amar Singh Rathore.

This favorite commander of the Emperor
Shah Jahan, once having overstayed his
leave, was insulted on his return by the King's
jealous Vazir in front of the assembled court.
He drew his sword, felled the Vazir, and
escaped, but was treacherously caught and
killed by his brother-in-law.

When the curtain rises on the play—
of 52 puppets—the stage, i.e. the assembly
hall, is empty and slowly fills with courtiers,
commanders and the Emperor who watch
the performance of plays within the play.

44 Two-Faced Puppet
Jaipur, Rajasthan
Wood, carved and painted, and cloth; h: 1'11"
20th century
Pamela Bull, Villanova, Pennsylvania

Cf. no. 43.

49
50

45 Head of a Puppet
Jaipur, Rajasthan
Wood, unpainted; 7½″ x 2½″
20th century
Crafts Museum, New Delhi #M/7/2127 (37)

B. Gujarat (nos. 46-81)

46 Dipa-Lakshmi
Plates XX and XXI
North Gujarat
Brass; 1′6⅛″ x 9″
18th century
Anonymous

The lamp (dipa) held by the hands of this lamp bearer is now missing. A work of high competence in its relation of basic shapes.

47 Vessel
Bhil Tribe, Gujarat, or Khandesh, (Maharashtra)
Brass; 2″ x 1¾″
ca. 18th century
Anonymous

On the globular body of the vase the following are shown in relief: five male figures dancing, with hands joined and raised to shoulder height. But for the central figure which seems to have the face of an animal, they wear pots or crowns on their heads. To the right: a serpent, a square enclosure having re-entrant angles, a tree and five parallel bars, each set divided into six squares. Above them are sun and moon. Two small holes below the neck. Projected double rim on top, low cone-shaped base. According to word of mouth, the vessel was used for medical magic.

48 Memorial Tablet
Rani Paraj, Surat, Gujarat
Stone; 10⅗″ x 6⅗″ x 2⅕″
20th century
Haku Shah, Ahmedabad

After a death, a man in trance paints an effigy of the deceased in orange colour on the black stone tablet which the spirit of the dead is believed to inhabit henceforward.

49 Architectural Fragment
Kutch, Gujarat
Wood, traces of paint; h: 1′10¼″
ca. 19th century
Vittorio Cacciandra, Bombay

A squatting female figure carved in relief supporting on her shoulders a standing male figure, carved in the round though equally planar in treatment.

50 Architectural Fragment: Tiger Hugging a Rabbit
Gujarat
Wood; 2′ x 4″
19th century
Crafts Museum, New Delhi #M/7/3814

51 Votive Horses and Their Riders
Bhil Tribe, Poshina, Sabarkantha, Gujarat
Terra-cotta; 3′1⅞″ x 1′4⅝″ x 10¾″, each
1966
Philadelphia Museum of Art, Philadelphia #67-197-1, 2, 3, 4

*52 Votive Horse and Rider
Bhil Tribe, Poshina, Sabarkantha, Gujarat
Terra-cotta; 2′7¾″ x 1′3″ x 7″
20th century
Harry Holtzman, Lyme, Connecticut

53 Horse and Rider
Rani Paraj, Surat, Gujarat
Terra-cotta; 1′¾″ x 7¼″ x 4¾″
20th century
Asutosh Museum of Indian Art, University of Calcutta #F.598

The verticalism of animal figurines like these, with their enormously long necks and fiercely held heads, is made the more striking by the scalloped edges forming the outer silhouette of the high, conical or tubular legs. The figurines are the work of the women of the local potter community and are made for tribal people. They are offerings to spirits who protect the field in fulfillment of vows.

Cf. Pupul Jayakar, "Terra-cotta Figurines from Tribal Gujarat," *Marg*, VII (1953), 27-32.

54 Horse
Rani Paraj, Surat, Gujarat
Terra-cotta; 9″ x 5½″ x 4″
20th century
Asutosh Museum of Indian Art, University of Calcutta #F.604

55 Horse
Rani Paraj, Surat, Gujarat
Terra-cotta, painted white; 1′6″ x 1′2″ x 7″
20th century
Crafts Museum, New Delhi #5/95

56 Two Horses
Godhara, Gujarat
Terra-cotta, with painted white spots; 5⅛″ x 2″
1966
Haku Shah, Ahmedabad

Offering to Sitala Devi and Balia Bapji, the goddess and god of smallpox.

57 Marriage Party (Toys)
Ahmedabad, Gujarat
Modelled clay, painted; 4¾″ x 1½″, each
1966
Philadelphia Museum of Art, Philadelphia #67-197-5

Figurines of musicians, bride and groom, guests bringing offerings, ritual objects. These gaily painted toys are the work of the Vaghari, or toymakers, who sell their goods in village and town.

51

58 Toys
Kutch, Gujarat
Modelled clay, painted; h: ca. 4″, each
1966
Philadelphia Museum of Art, Philadelphia
#67-197-6

Mother and child, woman with water pot,
cow and monkey, horseman, Ganesha,
peacock, sparrow, elephants, pets.

59 Malla Mata
Gujarat
Clay and cowry shells; 6″ x 2¾″ x 2⅓″
1966
Haku Shah, Ahmedabad

This shape of the Mother Goddess is
made by children in the Festival of
Nine Nights (Navaratri), of the Great
Goddess. It is a conical lump of clay with
the eyes and nose marked by cowry shells and
a large opening at the bottom which is the
"mouth" in which burns an oil lamp. The
children carry this light-goddess and collect
coins for the dead from passersby in the street.

60 A Painting Offered to Pithora
Bhil Tribe, Gujarat
Watercolour painting on paper; 3′ x 12′
1966
Haku Shah, Ahmedabad

Paintings like this are usually painted by
the Bhil on the walls of their houses in
fulfillment of vows for the good of the
unmarried girl in the house, or of the cattle,
or for good crops. They are offered to the
god Pithora. His image and that of other
gods, figures such as King Bhoja (who ruled
in the 11th century), figures of tiger, horse
and cow, birds and vehicles, including
aeroplanes, figures of intercourse and those of
sun and moon are distributed in free
rhythms on the white ground.

61 Torana
Saurashtra, Gujarat
Silk floss embroidery on cotton; 10″ x 3′5″
19th century
Philadelphia Museum of Art, Philadelphia
#66-189-8

Upper part of door frame hanging.
Lakshmi, the goddess "Luck", four armed,
seated, flanked by two elephants and two
horses, the ground completely covered with
embroidery using satin stitch, chain
stitch and interlocking stitch.

62 Wall Hanging (Pachhitpati)
Saurashtra, Gujarat
Silk floss embroidery on cotton; 4′1″ x 12′8″
Mid-19th century
Published: J. M. Nanavati, M. P. Vora
and M. A. Dhaky, *The Embroidery and
Bead Work of Kutch and Saurashtra*,
Department of Archaeology (Gujarat:
1966), Plate 44, p. 50.
Gandhi Smriti, Bhavnagar

The gable-shaped, bluish grey, handspun,
handwoven cotton cloth is embroidered
with figures of the participants in a marriage
procession to the house of the bride's
father. The bride is seen in the upper storey
of the house worshipping the goddess
Kalika. Musicians in lower storey. The
bridegroom afoot, under a canopy, the
others on elephants, in carriages and
palanquin. Ladies of the house, and others
come to welcome the groom. The hanging
decorated the triangular section of the
wall of a room with a gable roof.

63 Wall Hanging (Besan)
Saurashtra, Gujarat
Silk embroidery on silk; 4′ x 17′
19th century
Nirubhai Desai, Ahmedabad

64 Wall Hanging (Pachhitpati)
Saurashtra, Gujarat
Silk embroidery on cotton; 8″ x 17′4¾″
19th century
Haku Shah, Ahmedabad

The long textile decorated, like a frieze,
three or four of the walls of a room.
It is embroidered with figures of horsemen,
elephants, camels, carts, etc. Red, yellow
and green on blue ground.

65 Wall Hanging (Pachhitpati)
(part only)
Saurashtra, Gujarat
Silk embroidery on cotton; 9½″ x 4′5″
19th century
Haku Shah, Amedabad

Red and yellow figures of women with pots,
churning butter, etc.; blue ground.

66 Wall Hanging (Pachhitpati)
(part only)
Saurashtra, Gujarat
Silk embroidery on cotton; 1′3¾″ x 8′½″
19th century
Haku Shah, Ahmedabad

Tiger, birds, camel, women with pots.

67 Wall Hanging (Pachhitpati)
(part only)
Saurashtra, Gujarat
Silk embroidery on cotton; 9½″ x 4′4″
19th century
Haku Shah, Ahmedabad

68 Coverlet
Saurashtra, Gujarat
Silk embroidery on cotton; 7′7″ x 4′9″
19th century
Anonymous

Life trees and wheels, with peacocks and
parrots perching on them, show Mughal
influence and alternate with the solid colours
of elephants with their mahouts, cows,
guards, women churning butter, tigers,
monkeys, antelopes and rabbits. Border of
wave and life tree design. White ground.

73
―
78

69 Coverlet
Saurashtra, Gujarat
Cotton cloth embroidered with silk thread;
7' x 4'9"
19th century
Mrs. Shrimati Tagore, Calcutta

Cf. no. 68.

70 Coverlet
Saurashtra, Gujarat
Silk embroidery on silk; 2'¼" x 1'7¼"
19th century
Collection: Master Benjamin Marks

Animals, female attendants and flowers,
in single square compartments. Cf. no. 63.

71 Coverlet
Saurashtra, Gujarat
Silk embroidery on cotton; 3'10" x 2'11"
20th century
Philadelphia Museum of Art, Philadelphia
#65-200-13

"Tigers" and elephants in square
compartments, divided by chessboard
borders, framed by a floral motif.

72 Ganesha Sthapana
Saurashtra, Gujarat
Yellow cotton cloth embroidered with
silk thread; 1'2" x 1'
20th century
Mrs. Shrimati Tagore, Calcutta

Ceremonial wall hanging showing Ganesha,
the Lord of Success, flanked by two
acolytes. A wall hanging of this kind is
worshipped by bride and groom at their
wedding. The shape of a Ganesha Sthapana
corresponds to the longitudinal section
of a gabled shrine. Cf. nos. 73-77.

73 Ganesha Sthapana
Saurashtra, Gujarat
Yellow cotton cloth, embroidered;
1'9½" x 1'8½"
20th century
Philadelphia Museum of Art, Philadelphia
#65-200-8

74 Ganesha Sthapana
Saurashtra, Gujarat
Yellow cotton cloth, embroidered;
1'7½" x 1'7¾"
20th century
Philadelphia Museum of Art, Philadelphia
#65-200-9

75 Ganesha Sthapana
Saurashtra, Gujarat
Yellow cotton cloth, embroidered;
1'10½" x 1'8¾"
20th century
Philadelphia Museum of Art, Philadelphia
#65-200-10

76 Ganesha Sthapana
Saurashtra, Gujarat
Yellow cotton cloth, embroidered;
2'1" x 1'9½"
20th century
Philadelphia Museum of Art, Philadelphia
#65-200-11

77 Ganesha Sthapana
Saurashtra, Gujarat
Yellow cotton cloth, embroidered;
2' x 1'10½"
20th century
Philadelphia Museum of Art, Philadelphia
#65-200-12

78 Canopy
Saurashtra, Gujarat
Cotton appliqué on cotton; 13' x 10'3"
19th century
Courtesy Trustees of the Prince of Wales
Museum of Western India, Bombay #60.1

Rows of figures, grooms leading horses,
chariots, elephants with riders, birds,
shrine, deer, trees, etc., on white ground.

79 Coverlet
Saurashtra, Gujarat
Cotton appliqué on cotton; 2'7" x 2'6¾"
2nd quarter 20th century
Philadelphia Museum of Art, Philadelphia
#65-200-6

The symmetrical patterns are produced
by folding the cloth. Animal shapes, i.e.
elephant and bird, coalesced with
geometrical and freely curved surfaces into
an all over design distinguish this work
by Mahajan women. Here, as in the Bengal
Kantha (nos. 414-445) style and technique
reinforce one another creatively.

Cf. J. M. Nanavati, *op. cit.*, p. 30.

80 Coverlet
Saurashtra, Gujarat
Cotton appliqué on cotton; 3'8½" x 2'2¾"
2nd quarter 20th century
Philadelphia Museum of Art, Philadelphia
#65-200-7

81 Torana
Saurashtra, Gujarat
Cotton and silk cloth appliqué on cotton;
1'9" x 2'
20th century
Mrs. Shrimati Tagore, Calcutta

Ceremonial entrance hanging, with human
figures, elephants, birds, and floral motifs.

III Southern India (nos. 82-142)

A. Madras (nos. 82-112)

82 Equestrian Figurine
South India
Brass; 8″ x 6½″ x 3″
17th century
Anonymous

83 Equestrian Figurine
South India
Brass; h: 6″
17th-18th century
William H. Wolff, New York

84 Karuppan
South India
Brass; h: 6¾″
ca. 17th century
William H. Wolff, New York

The "dark god" holds in his raised right hand a curved knife and rests his left hand on a club-shaped staff, a dagger fastened to his waist, the lithe, richly bejewelled figure has wide-open, bulging eyes.

85 Warrior
South India
Brass; 5⅛″ x 2⁷⁄₁₆″
13th-16th century (?)
Nalini and Haridas K. Swali

This unusual figurine, standing straight with the right arm raised and the hand extended forward, the left arm pendent and holding a discus, is richly costumed and bejewelled. A scabbard and a dagger are attached to the belt.

86 Grama-Devata
South India
Brass, hollow cast; 6¾″ x 2⅛″ x ¾″
18th century
Anonymous

Village god holding short staff encoiled by serpent. A village god is a deity worshipped by the people living in a village, though not necessarily by all the people of the village.

87 Yashoda and Krishna
South India
Brass; h: 5⅞″
18th century
William H. Wolff, New York

The Krishna child, sprawling on his mother's right hip, drinks from her breast. Standing straight, she holds a flower in her raised right hand, the left hand rests on her hip.

88 Yashoda and Krishna
Pudukkottai, Madras
Brass, hollow cast; h: 5½″
ca. 18th century
Vittorio Cacciandra, Milan

89 Demon
Plate XXII
South India
Brass; 1′1½″ x 5¼″ x 5″
ca. 17th century
J. J. Klejman, New York

The expressive pattern produced by a particular technique of casting (broad strips of wax or resin over a core) combined with the naturalism of the underlying features and the surface treatment of the face is as unusual as the result is consistent.

90 Bird from an Oil Lamp
South India
Brass; h: 5¾″
ca. 17th century
Anonymous

With punched and engraved ornament.

91 Bird from an Oil Lamp
South India
Bronze; h: 6½″
ca. 18th century
Anonymous

Peacock with globe-shaped body.

92 Bird from an Oil Lamp
South India
Bronze; h: 9″
18th-19th century
Anonymous

93 Parrot
South India
Brass; 2¼″ x 3¼″
18th century
Anonymous

From a small oil lamp.

94 Parrot
South India
Brass; 1¾″ x 3¾″
18th century
Anonymous

From a small oil lamp.

95 Parrot
South India
Brass; 1⅞″ x 3⅛″
18th century
Anonymous

From a small oil lamp.

96 Hamsa (Wild Goose)
South India
Brass; 1¾″ x 3¾″
18th century
Anonymous

From a small oil lamp.

79
—
82

97 Hamsa (Wild Goose)
South India
Brass; 1¾″ x 3¾″
18th century
Anonymous

From a small oil lamp.

98 The Wives of the Rishis
South India
Wood carving; 1′7½″ x 1′¾″
19th century
Philadelphia Museum of Art, Philadelphia
#65-183-1

While the vast majority of the sculptures
which formed part of South Indian temple
cars conform with the shape of temple
sculptures in stone of the respective periods,
they have little of the directness and
spontaneity of rural art, as shown here.

99 Nandi
South India
Painted wood, sculpture in the round;
11″ x 1′1″ x 6″
19th century
Mrs. J. L. Eastwick, Charlestown,
Pennsylvania

100

100 Demon
South India
Terra-cotta; 1′7¾″ x 8¾″ x 6¼″
20th century
Haku Shah, Ahmedabad

A work of tribal character heightening the
power of the head and the extremities by
the tubelike shape of their carriers. The
projection of the feet from body and stand
is significant; it is also found in wood
sculptures from Bengal (no. 332).

*101A, B Two Circular Plaques
Representing Heads of Demons
A Shrine of Muniapan; Palladam, Coimbatore
B Shrine of Mariamman; Udamalpet,
   Coimbatore
Painted terra-cotta; diam. 9″ and 10½″
20th century
Harry Holtzman, Lyme, Connecticut

*102 Votive Horse
Tindivanum
Terra-cotta; 2′8½″ x 2′1″ x 9½″
20th century
Harry Holtzman, Lyme, Connecticut

*103 Four Votive Figures
One each from Madura, Viralimalai,
Tiruchirapalli and Pudukkottai
Terra-cotta; h: 1′6″; 1′5¾″; 11½″ and 11″,
respectively
20th century
Harry Holtzman, Lyme, Connecticut

*104 Crawling Figure
Madura
Terra-cotta; h: 11½″
20th century
Harry Holtzman, Lyme, Connecticut

*105 Heads of Heroes, Demons
and Devotees
One each from Tiruchirapalli and
Pudukkottai, two each from Madura
and Coimbatore
Terra-cotta; h: 9½″; 8″; 7¾″; 6¾″; 9″
and 8″, respectively
20th century
Harry Holtzman, Lyme, Connecticut

*106 Votive Bull
Tiruchirapalli
Terra-cotta; h: 1′½″
20th century
Harry Holtzman, Lyme, Connecticut

*107 Head of Bull
Madura
Terra-cotta; h: 5¾″
20th cenutry
Harry Holtzman, Lyme, Connecticut

*108 Votive Horse
Pudukkottai
Terra-cotta; h: 5½″
20th century
Harry Holtzman, Lyme, Connecticut

*109 Dog
Pudukkottai
Terra-cotta; h: 11″
20th century
Harry Holtzman, Lyme, Connecticut

*110 Bird
Coimbatore
Terra-cotta; h: 8″
20th century
Harry Holtzman, Lyme, Connecticut

*111 Votive Plaque
Wandiwash
Terra-cotta; h: 1′
20th century
Harry Holtzman, Lyme, Connecticut

Human figure on plain ground, arms
extended and raised to shoulder height, legs
distended in birth-giving position.

112 A Picture To Be Looked At
in the Morning
Tanjore, South India
Painting on wood, with mirror inset;
1′1¾″ x 11¼″
19th century
Philadelphia Museum of Art,
Philadelphia #65-200-1

In the centre of the picture is a king riding
an elephant shown in profile. Below the
elephant, inset against the cinnamon-coloured
earth and blue sky, is a rectangular mirror
framed in gold. The elephant's trunk is
embraced by a naked fool; the elephant's tail
is clasped by a black langur. All but the
elephant look out of the picture towards the
beholder who also sees his own face in
the mirror.

A safeguard against seeing an unfortunate face in the morning, is to look at one's own face in the mirror (Sayyid Khairayat Ahmad, "Omens in Bihar," *Indian Antiquary*, XIX [1890], 31). To avert evil a man may deliberately look at his own reflection (Abbot, *op. cit.*, p. 30). The elephant and the king who tower above the mirror in the total picture, may further strengthen the salutary effect of this morning ritual, brought about with the aid of Western painting on the level of a signboard painting.

B. Maisur (Mysore) (nos. 113-121)

113 Bull-Headed Deity
Plate 25
Basrur, Mundapur, Mangalore, Maisur
Wood sculpture in the round;
5'10" x 1'5" x 1'5"
ca. 18th century
Crafts Museum, New Delhi #M/7/3962

The image is one of a number of human or animal-headed statues which were part of a sanctuary in the heart of a forest called Mekkekappu. The figures are attendants of the protecting deity of the village. Cf. nos. 114-116.

114 Female Attendant Deity
Basrur, Mundapur, Mangalore, Maisur
Wood sculpture in the round;
5'10" x 1'5" x 1'5"
ca. 18th century
Crafts Museum, New Delhi #M/7/3960

The sculpture combines a majestic, classically Indian bust with a pillar shape for the rest of the body.

115 Female Attendant Deity
Basrur, Mundapur, Mangalore, Maisur
Wood; 6' x 1'5" x 1'5"
ca. 18th century
Crafts Museum, New Delhi #M/7/3961

116 Attendant Deity
Basrur, Mundapur, Mangalore, Maisur
Wood; 6' x 1'5" x 1'5"
ca. 18th century
Crafts Museum, New Delhi #M/7/3957

117 Vishnu
Maisur
Gouache and gold on paper; 10¼" x 7¼"
18th century
Philadelphia Museum of Art, Philadelphia #67-80-2

Standing image of Vishnu, Lakshmi seated at his feet holding up lotuses.

118 Vishnu as Man-Lion, and Consort
Maisur
Gouache on paper; 10¼" x 7¼"
18th century
Philadelphia Museum of Art, Philadelphia #67-80-3

113

114

119
———
126

119 Vishnu as Mohini
Maisur
Gouache and gold on paper; 10¾″ x 7⅞″
18th century
Anonymous

The hypnotic stare of the eyes of the
deity is underscored by the wide-open eyes
of the Kirttimukha or face of glory,
the monster head on top of the arch, and
of the bird-shaped Makaras, placed
on lateral consoles.

Note the twist to the left of the feet,
the tension of the lower part of the body,
the curves of the garment, peculiar to this
school which is related to the art of Kerala.

120A Vishnu Reclining on Ananta (Anantashayin)
(reverse of no. 120B)
Anonymous

120B Devotee
Maisur, South India
Gouache and gold on paper; 9¼″ x 6½″
18th century
Anonymous

The picture of the fashionably dressed
Bhakta has painted on its reverse the scene
of Vishnu slumbering on the world-serpent
Ananta while the demons Madhu and
Kaitabha arise from the flood (120A). The
paintings formed part of sequences of
paintings of the incarnations of Vishnu and of
scenes from the life of Krishna (nos. 117-121).

121 Krishna Triumphing Over
Saktasura, the "Stuck Demon"
Maisur
Gouache on paper; 10¼″ x 7¼″
18th century
Philadelphia Museum of Art, Philadelphia
#67-80-1

C. Kerala (nos. 122-142)

122 Shiva, Parvati and Devotees
Kerala
Brass; 4¼″ x 2″ x 1″
17th century (?)
C. L. Bharany, New Delhi

The seated divine group and the standing
devotees are aligned on a rectangular
pedestal. Style, physiognomy and costumes
are of a purely local type which distinguishes
the wood carvings (nos. 127-134). The Great
Tradition channelled through the historical
phases of South Indian art; from the Pallava
period onward, however, it was also
practiced in Kerala.

123 Aiyanar
Kerala
Brass; 3¾″ x 2½″ x 1½″
17th-18th century
Anonymous

124 Krishna, Venugopala
Kerala
Bronze; 3⅞″ x 1⅞″ x 1¼″
17th century
Anonymous

125 Bala Krishna
Kerala
Bronze; 2¾″ x 1½″ x 1½″
17th century
Anonymous

The child Krishna, standing with a
butter ball in each hand.

126 Lamp
Kerala
Brass; 9¼″ x 1′2⅞″
17th century
Anonymous

The lamp was carried on a staff. The
open oblong oil container with its
five circular sections for wicks rises from
a boat shape whose ends terminate in
peacocks' heads. It is supported on struts in
the shape of musicians playing on various
instruments and two Kirttimukhas on either
side of the sun-bird Garuda. Equestrian
figurines linking the oil container with the
peacocks' heads are the highest outposts of the
composition of this ritual implement. Shaft
and boat shape are connected by an
inverted, pointed arch set with flames and
allowing for two flying ganders (hamsa)
between shaft and arch. The Hamsas indicate
that the "boat" sails in the celestial region,
in which the horsemen are at home.
Kudus, circular window shapes, occupied
each by a face, decorate the boat.
Pendents are suspended from boat and arch.

127 Vishnu Reclining on Ananta (Anantashayin)
Kerala
Wood carving with traces of polychromy;
1′9″ x 6′
ca. 1600
Collection of Mr. and Mrs. James Greene

Vishnu Ananatashayin, reclining on the
World Serpent whose hoods are his halo, on
the primeval ocean is God in his conditioned
subtle form. He is known as Vishnu in his
divisible form. His state of slumber
(yoganidra) is accompanied here by the
two large shapes of the goddesses Shri Devi
and Bhu Devi. Brahma is born from
his navel. Avatars of Vishnu, hosts of gods,
etc., are arranged in praise and homage
along his recumbent shape.

128 Durga Triumphing Over
Nishumbha
Kerala
Wood carving; 1′1½″ x 1′11½″
ca. 1600
Philadelphia Museum of Art, Philadelphia
#65-29-1

128
—
138

129 Scenes from the Mahabharata
Kerala
Polychrome wood carving; 1'4" x 7'7½"
ca. 1600
Philadelphia Museum of Art, Philadelphia
#66-115-1

130 Scenes from the Mahabharata
Kerala
Polychrome wood carving; 1'1" x 6'6"
ca. 1600
Mr. and Mrs. Thomas C. Dove

131 Scenes from the Ramayana
Kerala
Polychrome wood carving; 1'2" x 5'9½"
ca. 1600
Philadelphia Museum of Art, Philadelphia
#66-115-2

132 Vastra-Harana
Kerala
Polychrome wood carvings; 6'7" x 1'1¼",
each panel
18th century
Mr. and Mrs. Thomas C. Dove

Lateral panels forming a perforated
screen, adjacent to the entrance of the
sanctuary of a temple car as built in Kerala.
The milkmaids, bereft of their clothing,
appear in three tiers and are shown
in rites of tree-climbing, below the
large flute-playing Krishna in the branches
of the tree on which their clothes are hung up
which he has stolen from them. Decorative
style in comparison with nos. 127-131.

133-134 Two Dvarapalas
Kerala
Polychrome wood carvings; 3'8" x 10½" each
18th century
Mr. and Mrs. Thomas C. Dove

These guardians of the entrance of the shrine
of a temple car were part of a screen.
Their forearms, however, project
three-dimensionally.

135 Mask of Gulikan
Kerala
Wood, covered with metallic paper; 2' x 1'6"
1966
Clifford R. Jones, Rochester, New York

God Gulikan is worshipped by the washermen
(Malayan) community of Malabar.

136 Garuda
Haripad Temple, Kerala
Stained wood, sculpture in the round;
h: 1'1¼"
Late 19th to early 20th century
Anonymous

The Sun Bird in human shape has a
beak, and a body midway between man
and bird. Hands joined in salutation.
A similar figure of Garuda is carved each
year for the annual rite of installing
the temple flag (dhvaja-pratishtha) and is
discarded afterwards.

**137 Figure for Black Magic
(Mantravada)**
Kerala
Wood, nails, thread; 7" x 2" x 1¾"
1966
Clifford R. Jones, Rochester, New York

The thread is from the cloth worn by the
person on whom the black magic is
to work. Such a figurine would be superficially
buried where it is expected the person will
step on it and feel the full effect of
the black magic.

**138-142 Figures from Shadow Plays of
the Ramayana**

---

138 Sita
Kerala
Buffalo skin, perforated and painted;
1'11" x 1'8¼"
20th century
Anonymous

Sita, the heroine of the Ramayana,
surrounded by parrots and creepers, seated
in her bower in the forest. Only one arm
of this figure is moveable in its three joints.
Below, a crow is shown thrice, pecking
at a breast cf. Ramayana, v, ch. 27. The
colours, black, red and yellow, are indelible.

139 Vibhishana
Kerala
Buffalo skin; 1'6½" x 10"
20th century
Government Museum, Madras #59/41

Younger brother of Ravana, the demon
king, who abducted Sita, the wife of Rama,
but is himself a devotee of Rama.

140 Atikaya
Kerala
Buffalo skin; 2'3" x 1'6½"
20th century
Government Museum, Madras #71/41

The "huge bodied," a Rakshasa or ogre,
holding a battle-axe. He is the son
of Ravana and fought against Rama, though
in his heart he was devoted to Rama.

141 Mandodari
Kerala
Buffalo skin; 1'10½" x 1'11½"
20th century
Government Museum, Madras #69/41

Wife of the demon king Ravana. It is
said that Sita was her daughter whom she
conceived after having drunk the blood
of the Rishis killed by Ravana. According to
a Jain account however (Gunabhadra
Acharya, 8th century), Ravana was her father.
A trident in the left hand of Mandodari,
a buffalo banner behind her left elbow.

142 Bali
Kerala
Buffalo skin, perforated and painted;
2'7½" x 1'3½"
20th century
Craig Makler, Philadelphia

The Monkey King who was slain by Rama.

145

IV Mid-India (nos. 143-188)

A. Madhya Pradesh (nos. 143-158)

143 Equestrian Figurine
Malwa, Madhya Pradesh
Brass; 3⅜" x 3⅛" x 1⅜"
18th century
Anonymous

Heavy-bodied horse with elaborated mane,
very short legs, knees bent. Rider holds
shield in one hand and wears a turban.

144 Ganesha
Madhya Pradesh
Brass, sculpture in the round; 4½" x 2"
19th century
C. L. Bharany, New Delhi

Ganesha seated with legs crossed on his
large Vahana, the mouse. Circular pedestal.
Asymmetrical disposition of masses and voids.

145 Dampati
Bastar, Madhya Pradesh
Bronze; 1'4" x 5"
ca. 19th century
Crafts Museum, New Delhi #M/7/3323

A donor couple, two householders, each
separately cast, the female figure carrying
two vessels. The "ornaments" worn on
the shoulders, encircling the arms are
noteworthy, also those worn on hips and
thighs. The male figure wears the
sacred thread.

146 Deity and Consorts
Bastar, Madhya Pradesh
Copper, sculpture in the round; 6½" x 3¼"
ca. 18th century
Manu Narang, Bombay

The tall central male figure holding sword
and shield, in line with him are his
consorts. They wear peaked crowns and
a Langoti as the only garment. long pendents
falling from the belt to the thighs. In front
of them are three firepits, a horse and
a dog. Cross cutout in the middle of the socle.

147 Elephant Rider (Ancestral Image)
Plate x
Jagdalpur, Bastar, Madhya Pradesh
Brass; 4¾" x 4¾" x 1½"
17th century
Anonymous

Sumptuously delicate spirals, raised dots,
parallels and twisted cords enliven the
surface texture of this unusual figurine. The

large rider is seated crosslegged in a
thronelike howda of which the uprights,
connected by straps, allow his whole figure
to be seen, showing a long tress dangling from
his crown along his concave back, the front
being covered by a triangular ornament.
In his raised right he holds a flower, in his
raised left a bowl (?). Spirals flank his head;
the high conical crown of dots or ringlets
is surmounted by projecting spirals.
The mahout, the elephant driver, of similar
appearance, lowers his mighty elephant
goad so that its point rests on the head of the
elephant. In his left he holds an oval fan (?)
on a long handle. The faces of both
the figures have wire loops outlining their
eyes and applied over their large conical
noses. A raised dot or flower enhances their
meeting. The mouth is an enormous curved
slit from ear to ear and is set with teeth.
The legs of the mahout dangle behind the
ears of the elephant. Their thin metal sheets
are decorated with raised dots. A large
circular head ornament and a large crescent
at the root of the tusks reinforce the shape of
the mouths of the riders. This group is
composed in a bold slanting ascent from
the sensitively curved tip of the elephant's
proboscis to the spiral crown of the rider.
The slim body of the elephant is streaked with
parallel, raised lines suggesting the folds
of its skin. The tail ends with a spike of
"hairs." The voids integrated in this
group are vitally part of the sculpture.

148 Horse
Jagdalpur, Bastar, Madhya Pradesh
Brass; 4¾" x 6¼"
17th century
J. J. Klejman, New York

But for the sensitively modelled head
the entire figurine is covered with plain
and twisted parallel wires.

149 Boar or "Unicorn"
Bastar, Madhya Pradesh
Brass; 2¾" x 3¼" x 2⅛"
18th century
Anonymous

Pleated band along center of back.
Three-dimensional knobs—bristles—cover
the body. A grooved curve from forehead to
jaws sets off the well-modelled face.
Horn on snout and in middle of forehead.

150 Incense Burner (Top)
Jagdalpur, Bastar, Madhya Pradesh
Brass; h: 4⅞"
ca. 18th century
Anonymous

Three-tiered, pyramidal, perforated roof
shape with cubical top opening on
four sides surmounted by a pot-shaped bird's
body. Large planar head and tail of bird.
Closely set plain and twisted wires
enhance the form.

151 Horse and Rider
Bastar, Madhya Pradesh
Terra-cotta; 9″ x 5″ x 7″
20th century
Crafts Museum, New Delhi #7/3170 (b)

152 Ceremonial "Doll"
Plate xxv
Muria Tribe, Bastar, Madhya Pradesh
Wood; 1′4½″ x 4¼″
20th century
Published: V. Elwin, *The Tribal Art of Middle India,* p. 118, Fig. 128.
National Museum, New Delhi #64.1405

The "doll" was attached to a wooden gong and used on dancing expeditions.

153 Mask
Plate xxx
Bhuiya Tribe, Bonai, Orissa – Madhya Pradesh border
Wood; 10⅞″ x 6¼″
20th century
Published: V. Elwin, *op. cit.,* Fig. 152.
National Museum, New Delhi #64.1306

Mask worn for divination.

154 Mask
Bhuiya Tribe, Orissa – Madhya Pradesh border
Wood; 11⅞″ x 6¾″
20th century
National Museum, New Delhi #64.1307

155 Mask
Bisonhorn Maria Tribe, Bastar, Madhya Pradesh
Wood, with hair affixed; 9¼″ x 6¼″
20th century
National Museum, New Delhi #64.1301

156 Mask
Plate xxxi
Bisonhorn Maria Tribe, Bastar, Madhya Pradesh
Wood, with hair affixed; 9¾″ x 6¼″
20th century
National Museum, New Delhi #64.1300

157 Mask
Baiga Tribe, Madhya Pradesh
Painted matting and peacock feathers;
2′10″ x 1′5″
Mid-20th century
Mrs. Aruna Vasudev, New Delhi

158 Mask
Baiga Tribe, Madhya Pradesh
Painted wood and peacock feathers;
3′2½″ x 11″
ca. 1960
Mrs. Aruna Vasudev, New Delhi

B. Maharashtra (nos. 159-181)

159 Equestrian Figurine
Bhil Tribe, Khandesh, Maharashtra
Brass; 4¼″ x 4″ x 1¾″
18th century
Anonymous

The short legged, heavy headed horse with its long legged, heavy headed rider rests on a rectangular base. His mighty nose juts out in line with the forehead.

160 Ambika
Khandesh, Maharashtra
Brass; 4⅝″ x 3¼″ x 1½″
ca. 17th century
Nalini and Haridas K. Swali

Ambika is here the Great Goddess in her Jain form. Unjustly driven away by her husband she committed suicide and became a Yakshini. Her husband having lost her, also committed suicide and was reborn as a lion.

Here the goddess is shown on her altar, four armed, holding weapons, her older son on her lap, the lion at her feet. On the pedestal, in low relief, three camels walking.

161 Durga
Maharashtra
Brass, sculpture in the round; 3″ x 1⅞″ x 1⅝″
18th century
Anonymous

The goddess riding on her lion has a squat stool for a pedestal.

162 Durga Killing the Buffalo Demon (Mahishasuramardini)
Nasik, Maharashtra
Brass; 4″ x 2½″ x 1¾″
18th-19th century
Anonymous

The background of the stele is made of flat strips and throws into relief the image. From the killed buffalo, his chest flat on the ground, emerges the head of the demon on an enormously long neck. Together with the trident of the goddess, its shape introduces an asymmetry intensifying the movement of the goddess.

163 Khandoba
Maharashtra
Brass; 4⅞″ x 4″ x 2″
18th century
Anonymous

This equestrian figurine represents Khandoba, a form of Shiva worshipped in Maharashtra. Slablike body; long, stiffly pendent legs. Horse flanked by two dogs. The group is mounted on a flat base.

164 Khandoba and Murli
Maharashtra
Brass; 3¼″ x 3½″ x 1¾″
ca. 17th century
Anonymous

Khandoba and Murli, his bride, ride stiff legged on one and the same horse. It stands on a flat metal base.

165 Charana Cha Tanda
Nasik, Maharashtra
Brass; 2″ x 7⅔″ x 1″
ca. 18th century
Nalini and Haridas K. Swali

Five bullocks being driven to a watering trough. If a group like this is offered to the spirits in their fields, the peasants believe this will bring them richer crops.*

*Information obtained by Haridas K. Swali.

166 Worship of the Linga
Nasik, Maharashtra
Brass; 1¾″ x 4⅛″
19th century
Anonymous

Circle of crowned worshipping gods, amongst them Ganesha, facing a Shiva-linga, with a rearing serpent behind it, in the centre. Water outlet in the shape of a bull's head in front. A fretted, low base frames and supports the circular platform.

167 Five-Headed Shiva (Panchamukhi)
Nasik, Maharashtra
Brass; 3″ x 3″ x 1½″
19th century
Anonymous

The figure holds sword and shield. Over the heads, forming an arc, is laid a wavy band; streamer-like supports for the arms are part of the design of the statuette.

168 Five-Headed Shiva (Panchamukhi)
Nasik, Maharashtra
Brass; 4¾″ x 2⅞″ x 3¼″
ca. 18th century
Anonymous

The heads form an array of triangular nose peaks. The body is a plane parallel to the back of the stele and has two balls for breasts. The two legs and hands (one broken) show their large five toes and fingers. The right hand holds a staff. The shape of the flamelike five crowns and of the finial of the stele are repeated at its bottom, right and left, by Panchamukhi shapes.

169 Five-Headed Shiva (Panchamukhi)
Nasik, Maharashtra
Lead; h: 1⅞″
18th century
Vittorio Cacciandra, Bombay

Shiva holding sword and shield, astride his "bull."

98

172
176

170 Shiva
Nasik, Maharashtra
Lead; h: 2¼″
18th century
Vittorio Cacciandra, Bombay

One-headed image.

171 Shiva
Nasik, Maharashtra
Lead; h: 2″
18th century
Vittorio Cacciandra, Bombay

Cf. no. 170.

172 The Great Ram
Nasik, Maharashtra
Brass; 5¼″ x 5½″ x 5″
19th century
Anonymous

The ram is practically one and a half
times as high as the crowned shepherd
who leads it. He carries a staff and a lamb
under his arm and is followed by a
sheep and two dogs. In front, on the left,
Nandi, offerings, and a Shiva-linga
surmounted by a serpent. On the left side, on
the floor: sun and moon symbolize the
everlasting remembrance of the deed, the
fulfillment of which this sculpture portrays.

Inscription on body of ram: "rajeshri
banajiba prasruta bapaji prarukta."
"As Bapaji said and as heard by Banaji."
This may refer to a vow.

173 Elephant and Rider
Nasik, Maharashtra
Brass; 3⅛″ x 2¾″ x 2″
18th century
Anonymous

The group is mounted on wheels.

**174 Seated Woman (Parvati?)
Holding a Child**
Maharashtra
Brass, sculpture in the round; h: 1⅝″
ca. 18th century
Vittorio Cacciandra, Bombay

The child (Ganesha?) against the woman's
chest. Broad, roundly modelled shoulders
and arms, covered by a short-sleeved
ornamental bodice, large circular earrings;
the figure holds with both hands a shallow
bowl with offerings.

175 Bird, from an Oil Lamp
Maharashtra
Brass; h: 5″
16th-18th century
Anonymous

176 Scrubber (Vajri)
South Maharashtra
Brass; 5¼″ x 6⅜″ x 2⅜″
19th century
Nalini and Haridas K. Swali

Hamsa (goose) feeding its young.
Scrubbers for cleaning the skin have been
used in India from the days of Mohenjo-Daro.
In Maharashtra they are topped by
sculptural handles.

**177 Painting from a Mahabharata
Series**
Paithan, Maharashtra
Earth colours on paper; 11⅞″ x 1′4¾″
Early 19th century
Anonymous

**178 Painting from a Mahabharata
Series**
Paithan, Maharashtra
Earth colours on paper; 11½″ x 1′5½″
Early 19th century
Mildred and W. G. Archer Collection #129

Two mounted warriors attacking a tiger.
Scene from the *Pandavapratapa* by Shridar,
a Marathi poem recounting the episode
of Yudhisthira's horse sacrifice.

Cf. P. J. Chinmulgund, "Paithan Painting,"
Times of India Annual, 1962, pp. 67-72.

**179 Painting from a Mahabharata
Series**
Paithan, Maharashtra
Earth colours on paper; 10″ x 1′3½″
Early 19th century
C. L. Bharany, New Delhi

180 Painting from a Ramayana Series
Paithan, Maharashtra
Earth colours on paper; 11″ x 1′3½″
Early 19th century
Anonymous

181 Painting from a Ramayana Series
Paithan, Maharashtra
Earth colours on paper; 11″ x 1′3½″
Early 19th century
Anonymous

The paintings from Paithan (nos. 177-181)
are epic in content and form. Although they
were painted in the early nineteenth century,
they seem cast in one mould with the
ancient, heroic themes.

C. Andhra Pradesh (nos. 182-188)

182 Shadow Play Puppet: Sita
Plate XXIX
Andhra Pradesh
Leather, cut, painted and oiled; 4' x 2'4"
1st half 19th century
Crafts Museum, New Delhi #M/13/386

The puppet is from a Ramayana set of
a Tholu Bommalata or "leather figurine
puppet play." The figurines are manipulated
on bamboo sticks. Each Bommalata
troupe produced its own figures for its own
use. Deer or goatskin painted red, yellow,
green and black and made semi-transparent
by oiling is punched so that the light
shines across the punched patterns. It is shed
by two lamps, one and a half to two feet
behind the screen. The puppets are
held close to it. The figures appear and
disappear once they are taken beyond the
range of the light. The shadow plays are
staged as part of the rites of spring. A lamp
which is lit from the inner shrine of the
temple and the storytellers who are also the
puppet players are escorted from the
temple to the playhouse where the footlights
are lit from the light from the temple.*

*Census of India, 1961, Vol. II, Pt. VII. A (1),
"Selected Crafts of Andhra Pradesh," pp. 19-35.

183 Shadow Play Puppet: Lion
Andhra Pradesh
Leather, cut, painted and oiled; 2'11" x 3'11"
1st half 19th century
Crafts Museum, New Delhi #M/13/386

184 Shadow Play Puppet: Horseman
Andhra Pradesh
Leather, cut, painted and oiled; 3'8" x 2'4"
1st half 19th century
Crafts Museum, New Delhi #M/13/386

185 Shadow Play Puppet: Nalini, the Dancer
Andhra Pradesh
Leather, cut, painted and oiled; 2'11" x 1'10"
1st half 19th century
Crafts Museum, New Delhi #M/13/386

186 Shadow Play Puppet: Hanuman
Andhra Pradesh
Leather, cut, painted and oiled; 3'10" x 2'10"
1st half 19th century
Crafts Museum, New Delhi #M/13/386

187 Shadow Play Puppet: Jester
Andhra Pradesh
Leather, cut, painted and oiled; 2'8" x 1'1"
1st half 19th century
Crafts Museum, New Delhi #M/13/386

188 Hookah Bowl in the Shape of a Tiger
Hyderabad, Andhra Pradesh
Brass, traces of gilding; 7½" x 9" x 3½"
ca. 17th century
Anonymous

Surviving Seljuk type endowed with
Indian expanding volume.

V Northern India (nos. 189-221)

189 Durga Killing the Buffalo Demon (Mahishasuramardini)
Plate XXXV
Panjab or Himachal Pradesh
Slate; 11" x 5¾" x ¾"
8th century
Anonymous

Perforated votive tablet.

For iconographically related images of
the 6th-8th century from Western and
Mid-India, see M. Seshadri, "Mahisasura
Mardini," The Half-Yearly Journal of
the Mysore University, Sect. A, Vol. XXII
(March, 1963), Plates 4 and 6a.

190 Votive Horse
Rupar, Panjab
Terra-cotta; 1'6" x 1' x 8'
Mid-16th-18th century
Crafts Museum, New Delhi #M/7/316

The body is a purely geometrical hollow
cylinder which strongly contrasts with the
delicately modelled head and legs.

Cf. Casal, J. M., Fouilles d'Amri (Paris,
1964), pp. 75, 158, #14.

191 Phulkari
Haryana
Cotton cloth embroidered with floss silk;
7'9" x 4'8"
ca. 1900
Philadelphia Museum of Art, Philadelphia
#67-211-1

Multicoloured figures of women carrying
water pots on their heads, women in chariots,
animals, large ornaments; starry flowers. A
"lotus" in the centre. Cf. nos. 414-445.

192 Toy
Shahpur, West Panjab (West Pakistan)
Wood; 7¾" x 10¾" x 8"
19th century
Victoria and Albert Museum, London
#I.S.2397-1883

A bird and a young one on each side,
legs and tail on wheels. Lacquered in red,
green and black; engraved.

193 Krishna, Flute-Playing
Uttar Pradesh
Brass; 5" x 1¾" x 1½"
ca. 17th-18th century
Nalini and Haridas K. Swali

194

196 detail
196 detail
197

194 Boat (Toy)
Varanasi (Banaras), Uttar Pradesh
Painted wood; 4¼" x 8" x 2"
ca. 1940
Anonymous

Boat with prancing white horses in prow; stern in shape of crocodile head (makara) and carrying a kiosk in the centre. In a large boat of this type the Maharaja of Banaras conveyed on the river Ganges once a year, after the Festival of Lights, in order to watch a performance of Krishna subduing the serpent Kaliya.

195 Canopy
Plate XL
Bahraich, Uttar Pradesh
Appliquéd cotton cloth; 15'3" x 6'1"
Early 20th century
Exhibited: Exhibition of Indian Textiles, Museum of Modern Art, New York, May-July, 1955.
Published: *Textiles and Ornaments of India*, ed. Monroe Wheeler (New York, 1956), p. 28.
Mildred and W. G. Archer Collection #1

Six strips of red, white and blue cloth and two further strips, one with chevron pattern, the other striped. The appliquéd figures are: a shrine on top, women, sepoys, musicians, a standard bearer, parrots, peacocks, deer, fish, elephants (with and without riders), horses (with and without riders), tigers, including a tigress with her cub, leaves. The right-hand strip has mainly eight-petalled rosettes.

The shrine (durga) on top represents the tomb at Bahraich of the warrior-saint Saiyid Salar Masud, nephew of Mahmud of Ghazni. It is said to have been built in the 13th century. Saiyid Salar Masud invaded Oudh in ca. 1033 A.D. and was killed by the confederate Hindu chiefs.

Cloths of this type of canopy are offered every year to the shrine during a fair in May. At the end of each year old offerings are auctioned. When acquired in 1939, this cloth was being used as the canopy to a stall in the Sonepur Mela (fair).*

*From a note by W. G. Archer.

196 Canopy
Bahraich, Uttar Pradesh
Appliquéd cotton cloth; 8' x 5'
20th century
Collection, Dorothy Norman

The field is divided by appliquéd individual borders into fifteen panels, each having a composition of its own such as six club-swinging men in the first row; in the second row, a man carrying a sword and bag amid five bulls; a life tree behind a man flanked by two saddled animals, and a man holding circular objects, surrounded by six animals. Other panels have only animals confronted, or animals in profile with their riders—the entire figure of the rider shown in front view in front of the saddle; a scene of

catching large fish; a panel of birds stylized as large triangles; another life tree, completely different in its rendering from the one on top, with two confronting animals before it. Each panel has a sun with rays in each corner. The textile is said to have been given to the bride at her wedding.

197 Shivaite Panel
Kangra, Himachal Pradesh
Wood; 11½" x 10"
18th century
Courtesy Trustees of the Prince of Wales Museum of Western India, Bombay #658

The three horizontal panels show sixteen women hand in hand; two figures enthroned next to a tree on the right, three priests holding water vessels; a Shiva-linga on the left and four figures above sun and moon rosettes, on both ends. Between them various symbols based on the number four. Cow and calf, a squatting figure holding a bowl, two bowls on the ground, a square enclosure (pitha?) where a coiled shape emerges and seems to pass behind the steps which divide this scene from the figure of a warrior riding an elephant.

198 Ram
Kangra, Himachal Pradesh
Brass; 4" x 4½"
ca. 18th century
Mrs. Pupul Jayakar, New Delhi

Heavy basic shape with some "naturalistic" modelling; decorated with garlands, a flower on the head.

199 Garuda
Kangra, Himachal Pradesh
Brass; 4" x 1½"
18th century
Mrs. Pupul Jayakar, New Delhi

Kneeling figurine, part of its garment functions as support.

200 Boar
Kangra, Himachal Pradesh
Brass; 4½" x 4½"
ca. 18th century
Mrs. Pupul Jayakar, New Delhi

Standing on rings for insertion of crossbars for attachment of wheels.

201 Ganesha
Kulu, Himachal Pradesh
Brass sculpture in the round; 4" x 2½" x 1½"
15th-16th century
C. L. Bharany, New Delhi

Seated, serpent encoiled, modelled in continuity of the Great Tradition. A running mouse, his Vahana, at the feet of Ganesha.

199

202 Ganesha
Kulu, Himachal Pradesh
Brass; 6½" x 3⅜" x 1¾"
ca. 17th century
Anonymous

Ganesha here has not only the body but
also the face of a man. It is overlaid from
crown to chin by the elephant's trunk
which also grasps the ball of sweetmeat held
out by the god's upper left hand. The
other hands hold bell, axe and rosary. Above
the crown of Ganesha rises a large trident
(of Shiva). Serpent on circular base.

203 Ganesha
Kulu, Himachal Pradesh
Brass; 4¼" x 2¾"
18th century
C. L. Bharany, New Delhi

Arch-shaped frame of the stele, surmounted
by a "jewel" crest, rectangular pedestal
in wire-technique. Ganesha, two armed,
has the face of man, the sticklike trunk being
a connecting part between nose and
sweetmeats. The body has the shape of a
buckled shield set up on top of
serpent-like coiled legs.

204 Durga Slaying the Buffalo Demon
(Mahishasuramardini)
Kulu, Himachal Pradesh
Brass; 5¾" x 2¾" x 1½"
ca. 17th century
Nalini and Haridas K. Swali

205 Durga Slaying the Buffalo Demon
(Mahishasuramardini)
Plate XXXVI
Kulu, Himachal Pradesh
Brass; 5" x 4"
ca. 18th century
C. L. Bharany, New Delhi

The Great Goddess, eight armed and
victorious over the buffalo demon, is here
all face and arms, her small body planted
on the barrel shape of the buffalo's body which
runs parallel to the base of the pointed stele.
Her lion vehicle is on her right, continuing
the horizontal extent of the buffalo.
Cf. the masklike face of the Goddess
with masks nos. 210-212.

206 Durga and Attendants
Kulu, Himachal Pradesh
Brass; 3¼" x 3¼" x 1"
18th century
Anonymous

Upper part of back of stele broken.
The length of the face of the figurine
on the left, holding a Shiva-linga, exceeds
that of her body plus thighs.

207 Durga Slaying the Buffalo Demon
(Mahishasuramardini)
Kulu, Himachal Pradesh
Brass; h: 5"
ca. 18th century
Mrs. Pupul Jayakar, New Delhi

208 Lakshmi-Narayana on Garuda
Kulu, Himachal Pradesh
Brass; 6" x 2½" x 1⅞"
ca. 18th century
Anonymous

The deities are supported on head and
wings of the man-shaped body of the sun-bird.
Figures and frame of the stele are overlaid
with, or are translated into, wire shapes.
Lakshmi wears a veil over her head.

209 Shiva Enthroned
Kulu, Himachal Pradesh
Brass; 3¼" x 1" x ¾"
18th-19th century
Anonymous

Holding staff and drum (damaru);
wearing a very high crown (jata mukuta);
the body a thin sheet with three knobs
projecting for breasts and navel.
High, cubical pedestal.

210 Mask of Goddess
Kulu, Himachal Pradesh
Brass; 7" x 3½"
ca. 18th century
Vittorio Cacciandra, Milan

Figure of child on plaque.

211 Mask of Goddess
Kulu, Himachal Pradesh
Brass; 9" x 7⅜" x 3"
18th century
Mr. and Mrs. Earl Morse, New York City

Two serpents on plaque.

212 Mask of Goddess
Kulu, Himachal Pradesh
Brass; 6" x 3½"
18th-19th century
Vittorio Cacciandra, Milan

213 Coverlet (Rumal)
Chamba, Himachal Pradesh
Floss silk embroidery in satin stitch on cotton;
2'2" x 2'1"
18th century
Published: *Textiles and Ornaments of
India*, The Museum of Modern Art
(New York, 1956), p. 51.
The Metropolitan Museum of Art, New York
#31.82.4

Scenes from the Ramayana: at the bottom,
the bridge from India to Lanka (Ceylon),
Hanuman, the monkey chief having
covered the distance by one leap (shown
within the embroidered diagonal band); the
bears and monkeys which aided Rama
in his invasion of Lanka; Sita sitting in the
palace of Ravana facing the ten-headed
demon king.

212

214 Coverlet (Rumal)
Kangra, Himachal Pradesh
Silk embroidery on cotton; 1'10¼" x 3'8"
18th century
Philadelphia Museum of Art, Philadelphia
#67-207-1

In the central panel: The wedding of Shiva
and Parvati, with Brahma as priest,
and Ganesha present in the marriage tent;
a female figure, Menaka, behind the seated
couple. Outside the tent: women bringing
gifts, musicians, horse, elephant, cow,
peacocks, palanquin, chair, stool,
boxes and bed.

In each of the lateral panels: cypress
trees alternating with figures of girls, each
reaching out into the foliage of a tree.

215 Coverlet (Rumal)
Mandi (?), Himachal Pradesh
Silk embroidery on cotton, 3'3½" x 3'3"
Late 18th to early 19th century
Anonymous

Divided into nine panels, the central one
occupied by two standing figures of similar
type, each holding objects in raised
hands. An animal in each of the four
squares in the corners.

216 Coverlet (Rumal)
Chamba, Himachal Pradesh
Silk embroidery on cotton; 2'1" x 1'11½"
19th century
Philadelphia Museum of Art, Philadelphia
#66-189-7

A composition of nine symmetrically
disposed Shikhara temples of local type,
their flags and peacocks, each temple showing
an image enshrined. The central Vishnu
temple shows on its Shikhara the
triple-headed deity as part of the sculptural
symbolism of local Hindu temples, but its
flags fly from lateral minarets. These
are replaced on the eight smaller temples by
three pots piled in the vertical, of
Hindu auspicious symbolism.

217 Coverlet: Rama, Sita and
Lakshmana in Exile
Himachal Pradesh
Silk embroidery on cotton; 2' x 3'2"
19th century
Anonymous

Framed by a floral border, Rama, with
his bow, followed by Sita and Lakshmana,
clad in leaves. The large size of Rama
stresses his importance, that of the
trees shows decorative intention.

218 Coverlet (Rumal)
Kulu, Himachal Pradesh
Silk embroidery on cotton; 1'11" x 1'11"
19th century
Anonymous

Radha and Krishna in a central ellipse,
surrounded by trees and birds.

219 Standing Figurine of Woman
Kashmir or Kulu
Brass; h: 6½"
ca. 18th century
Vittorio Cacciandra, Milan

Slablike body, wire-shaped limbs; the
skirt modelled along the leg-sticks; the
face retaining a "classical" air. A child
supported on the right hip.

220 Vishnu on Garuda
Kashmir
Brass; 8" x 5"
ca. 17th century
Manu Narang, Bombay

The sun-bird, a serpent in its beak, flanked
by serpent coils and with wings extended
to the hands of two-armed Vishnu is
linked with the large, crowned head of the
god by the short stem of Vishnu's body.
Residual, "classical" Western features
of the face.

221 Durga Slaying the Buffalo Demon
(Mahishasuramardini)
Kashmir
Brass; 9½" x 4½"
ca. 17th century
Manu Narang, Bombay

Here the breast-globes of the victorious
goddess are given their visual response by
the circular holes of the flat pediment
of her "shrine" which enframes her figure
which is all chest and head, supported
laterally by her wire-shaped arms, and
vertically by her diminutive shape, from the
waist down, encased in an ornamental,
wire-technique skirt.

Although nos. 222-223 are from Nuristan,
Afghanistan, they are in form and
conception part of the family of clay
and wooden, Hindu and tribal, equestrian
statuary made in India.

---

222 Memorial Figure of a Horseman
Nuristan, Afghanistan
Wood, partly painted; 1'7¼" x 11" x 4½"
ca. 1880
Victoria and Albert Museum, London
#I.S.4-1957

Wearing a unicorn headdress. Eyes inset
with white composition. The figure is said
to have come from Gilgit.

Tally for a life-size effigy. A year after the
rites for the dead have been performed, a
life-size equestrian statue, carved in wood
is set up on the grave, if the deceased
was a person of consequence, so that he
may ride his horse in afterlife.

Cf. Hackin, "Les Idoles du Kafiristan,"
Artibus Asiae, 1925, pp. 258-62.

223 Memorial Figure of a Horseman
Nuristan, Afghanistan
Wood, partly stained blue; 1'3¼" x 8" x 4"
Late 19th to early 20th century
Victoria and Albert Museum, London
#I.S.52-1952

The rider wears a peaked turban.

Tally for a life-size effigy. The horse on
which the figure may ride in afterlife
is a status symbol. Such tallies are usually
displayed in a village lane or outside
the deceased's house.*

Cf. A. Mookerjee, *Folk Art of Bengal*,
Plate 14; a miniature "Brisakat" from Sylhet.

*From a note, in the Victoria and Albert
Museum, by W. G. Archer.

VI Eastern India (nos. 224-470)

A. Bihar (nos. 224-283)

224 Indra (?)
Bihar
Brass; 9½" x 6½" x 4½"
18th century
Bion A. Bowman, Boston, Massachusetts

The crowned rider seated within a
mandorla-like arch on an elephant seems
to hold a vestigial thunderbolt (vajra) in his
right and a flower in his left hand. This
part of the sculpture is hinged on to
the back of the elephant which wears head
ornaments and fringed rug. The almond-
shaped plaques on its heavy, conical legs
indicate ornamentally the place of the joints.
Wheels missing.

225 Lakshmi Riding Her Owl
Bihar
Brass; 7" x 3¾" x 3½"
19th century
Anonymous

The wings of the owl are joined with the
arch-mandala of the goddess. The owl, the
Vahana, or vehicle of the goddess,
wears a nose ring.

226 Ganesha
Bihar
Brass; 8" x 4½"
18th-19th century
C. L. Bharany, New Delhi

Seated with legs pendent on a wickerwork
stool; a feline animal head (of his
mouse vehicle) protruding.

227 Ganesha
Bihar
Brass; 4⅞" x 2½" x 1⅞"
19th-20th century
Anonymous

Standing, the entire image being a
composition of round wires and flat streaked
bands; the former constituting the body
of Ganesha, the latter his hands, halo and

socle. The body of his vehicle, the mouse, is
a coiled streaked band having a
three-dimensional head projecting in front.
Above the spiral ears the flat, triangular
crown of Ganesha is the meeting place of
the various form units.

228 Equestrian Figurine
Plate xv
Bihar
Brass; 4½" x 4½" x 2½"
18th century
Anonymous

The body is cast in wire-technique
allowing the core to be seen between the
meshes in some places; on the neck of
the horse the wires are applied on the smooth
metal ground. The mane of the horse makes
a flaming pattern in lacy zigzag wires.
The thin, high legs are cast solid, the knees
being accentuated. The rider, cast solid, sits
on a saddle rising to a point at the back.
His arms are raised laterally; he does
not hold the reins, but brandishes in his right
a short sword and holds in his left a
diminutive shield facing upward. Peaked
nose, peaked hat, body roundly modelled.

229 Equestrian Figurine
Bihar
Brass; 5¼" x 5" x 3"
18th century
Anonymous

The horse has almost a camel's hump
and a foliate tail.

230 Equestrian Figurine
Bihar
Brass; 6" x 5½" x 3"
18th century
Anonymous

With both his hands the rider holds a gun.

231 Equestrian Figurine
Bihar
Brass; 4⅝" x 4¼" x 1¼"
18th century
Anonymous

Horse with very long body, short neck
and small head. The reins are slung around
the waist of the rider.

232 Antelope and Rider
Bihar
Brass; 4½" x 3¾" x 1½"
18th century
Anonymous

233 Antelope
Plate xvii
Bihar
Brass; 4½" x 3¼" x 2½"
18th century
Anonymous

Legs resting on rods to which wheels
were attached.

215 detail
217
218

234 Antelope
Plate XVIII
Bihar
Brass; 6″ x 5″ x 3⅛″
18th century
Anonymous

A large spur on the back, a transformation
of the wire ends of the necklace.
A pendent is affixed in front to the muzzle.

235 Antelope
Bihar
Brass; 5½″ x 4″ x 3″
18th century
Anonymous

236 Antelope
Bihar
Brass; 5½″ x 3½″ x 2⅞″
18th century
Anonymous

237 Stag or Antelope
Bihar
Brass; 4¼″ x 3½″ x 2½″
18th century
Anonymous

With nose-ring and ornament.

238 Two-Headed Antelope
Bihar
Brass; 3¼″ x 4″ x 2″
18th century
Anonymous

One head looking forward, the other back;
wheels missing.

239 Antelope
Bihar
Brass; 5½″ x 6″ x 2″
19th century
Anonymous

The body is perforated in parallel, cusped
rows. Spirals and rings respectively indicate
the joints of the sticklike legs. A rectangular
plate was hinged on the belly making this
figurine a container of camphor. Loop on
chest for string; wheels missing.

240 Antelope
Bihar
Brass; 3⅝″ x 3½″ x ¾″
18th century
Anonymous

Cast in two halves, the body serving
as a casket.

241 Antelope
Bihar
Brass; 4½″ x 3″ x 1″
18th century
Anonymous

Cast in two parts, hinged to serve as a
receptacle. The receptacle antelopes are
without rods and wheels.

242 Sheep
Bihar
Brass; 2¾″ x 3″ x 2″
19th century
Anonymous

The figurine has its basic shape covered
with closely set plain wires and parallel rows
of wire scallops suggestive of its curly wool.

243 Fish
Bihar
Brass; 3″ x 7½″
19th century
Anonymous

The body, a perforated, diagonal grille;
head pointed, having a nose and long, curved
brows. A tendril issues from its mouth.
Loop on back, for hanging; with part
of original chain.

244 Fish
Bihar
Brass; 3″ x 7″
19th century
Anonymous

With rounded head and long whiskers;
loop on back.

245 Fish on Wheels
Bihar
Brass; 8″ x 5″ x 2½″
19th century
Anonymous

A hinged metal plate on the underside.

246 Peacock
Bihar
Brass; 6″ x 3½″ x 2¼″
19th century
Anonymous

247 Peacock
Bihar
Brass; 4¾″ x 2½″ x 2¾″
19th century
Anonymous

Holding a snake in its beak.

248 Two Peacocks on a Perch
Bihar
Brass; 5⅜″ x 2¾″ x 2″
19th century
Anonymous

249 Receptacle
Bihar
Brass; 6¼″ x 3½″ x 3½″
19th century
Anonymous

Container on stand, the semicircular upper
lid crested by a peacock; four long,
young peacocks' necks emerging from the
lid in the four directions.

250 Receptacle
Bihar
Brass; 6″ x 2¾″ x 2¾″
19th century
Anonymous

In the shape of a pomegranate, hanging.
Shell of wires only, without core.

251 Lamp
Bihar
Brass; 4″ x 3⅜″ x 3⅜″
19th century
Anonymous

Stand encircled by serpent.

252 Lamp
Bihar
Brass; 3¾″ x 4¼″ x 3″
19th-20th century
Anonymous

Two feline animals, each holding up a ball
on its rim; a bird above the handle.

253 Dipa-Lakshmi
Ranchi, Bihar
Terra-cotta, painted; 1′1½″ x 6″
20th century
Asutosh Museum of Indian Art,
University of Calcutta #F.536

Conical lamp stand—with female bust
and head emerging—from which oil lamps
branch out like so many arms.

254 Milkmaid
Rajgir, Bihar
Painted clay; 7¼″ x 3⅛″
2nd part 20th century
Asutosh Museum of Indian Art,
University of Calcutta #T.992

255 Shiva and Parvati
Mongroni, Darbhanga, North Bihar
Clay, painted; 1′ x 7″ x 7″
1966
Crafts Museum, New Delhi #7/3945

256 Kamalban
Plate XLIV, (detail)
Darema, Darbhanga, North Bihar
Coloured ink on paper; 1′1″ x 1′4″
ca. 1920-1940
Mildred and W. G. Archer Collection #120

The Kamalban or "lotus forest" is a
symbolic design interspersed with birds,
fish and turtle, sun and moon and floral
devices. The central motif resembles the Bhu
mandal symbol of the Tara Vrata Alpona
in Bengal.* It is composed of a human
head on top, which there symbolizes the
sun, and a horizontal shape at the bottom,
the crescent of the moon. The corresponding
shape here, however, is linked by a
rectangle with the central vertical motif
which extends below and above the large
lotus circle in the centre. This large
lotus signifies the Earth. The Earth-lotus

symbol here has proliferated into a lotus forest of surrounding lotuses. At the bottom of the drawing is the bridegroom in his palanquin, and on the right are Shiva, Nandi and Parvati.

By a Maithil Kayasth woman from the house of Sabhapati Das.

*According to Mr. Archer, who collected on the spot the objects lent by him, the central device is a phallic symbol of a bamboo tree piercing a circle of lotus flowers.

257 Panel of Gods and Goddesses
Simri, Darbhanga, North Bihar
Coloured ink on paper; 11½" x 1'3¾"
ca. 1920-1940
Mildred and W. G. Archer Collection #126

The presence of the gods blesses the bridal couple.

By a Maithil Kayasth woman from the house of Sripati Mallik.

258 Maithil Brahman Bridegrooms
Madhubani, Darbhanga, North Bihar
Pen and ink on paper; 1'4" x 1'1"
ca. 1920-1940
Mildred and W. G. Archer Collection #103

A Maithil Brahman is a Brahman living in Mithila, the ancient name of North Bihar.

By a Maithil Brahman woman.

259 Maithil Brahman Brides
Madhubani, Darbhanga, Bihar
Pen and ink and watercolours; 1'1" x 1'4"
ca. 1920-1940
Mildred and W. G. Archer Collection #104

Parrots, which here form part of the design, are auspicious birds.

By a Maithil Brahman woman.

260 Bride Covering Her Face with Her Sari
Darema, Darbhanga, North Bihar
Watercolours; 1'2" x 11"
ca. 1880
Mildred and W. G. Archer Collection #109

By a Maithil Kayasth woman from the house of Sabhapati Das. Torn fragment.

261 Veiled Bride, with Fish and Parrot
Plate XXXVII
Darema, Darbhanga, North Bihar
Watercolours; 1'1" x 9"
ca. 1920-1930
Mildred and W. G. Archer Collection #111

By a Maithil Kayasth woman from the house of Sabhapati Das.

262 Fiddle
Plate XXV
Santal Tribe, Bihar
Wood; 2'9¼" x 9⅞" x 6¾"
19th-20th century
National Museum, New Delhi #64.1293

A rectangular panel with four dancers surmounts the "head" of the fiddle.

263 Humped Bull (Toy)
Bihar
Wood, painted; 8⅝" x 2⅜" x 4¼"
20th century
National Museum, New Delhi #64.1410

264 Marriage Litter (part)
Santal Tribe, Bihar
Wood; 4¼" x 11½"
1st half 20th century
National Museum, New Delhi #64.1284

Procession in low relief of men carrying bows, umbrellas (?); and animals, etc.

Cf. V. Elwin, *The Tribal Art of Middle India,* pp. 78-79, Figs. 83-85.

265 Santal Pat (section):
The Tiger-God
Salpatra, Jamtara, Santal Parganas, Bihar
Earth colours on paper; 1'3¾" x 1'1"
ca. 1920
Mildred and W. G. Archer Collection #316

The tiger-god, holding club and rosary. The tiger-god is sometimes shown as a Hindu and sometimes as a Moslem. The tiger has the spots of a leopard. The word "bagh" denotes both tiger and leopard. Tigers now have disappeared from the Santal Parganas. The tiger-god has spread from Bengal into the Santal Parganas.

By Jugal Chitrakara

266 Santal Pat (section)
Dumka, Santal Parganas, Bihar
Earth colours on paper; 1'5½" x 1'1"
ca. 1920
Mildred and W. G. Archer Collection #230

The tiger-god is variously known as Chand Bagar Kul, Baghaut Bonga, Satya Narayan Pir and Satya Pir.

267 Santal Pat (section)
Sonapuri, Dumka, Santal Parganas, Bihar
Earth colours on paper; 1'5½" x 1'1"
ca. 1920
Mildred and W. G. Archer Collection #188

The Great Waters before the creation of the Earth. Part of a scroll relating the story of the origin of the Santal tribe.

268 Santal Pat (section)
Dumka, Santal Parganas, Bihar
Earth colours on paper; 11" x 1'
ca. 1920
Mildred and W. G. Archer Collection #226

Two Moslems attending the shrine of the tiger-god (Satya Pir). A lamp burns on the top; a flag on either side. This is the second panel of a Moslem tiger-god scroll.

265

269 Santal Pat (section)
Dumka, Santal Parganas, Bihar
Earth colours on paper; 1'8½" x 8"
ca. 1920
Mildred and W. G. Archer Collection #232

Two scenes from a Yama Pat:

1. Yama, king of the dead, smoking a
hookah, and a sinner standing beside him.

2. A demon burns a man in a fire.

270 Santal Pat (section)
Pipla, Jamtara, Santal Parganas, Bihar
Earth colours on paper; 1'2½" x 9¼"
ca. 1930
Mildred and W. G. Archer Collection #312

Panel from a scroll telling the story of
the Santals. The killing and cutting up of the
python which Marang Buru, the Preserver,
is said to enjoy eating. Below, the feast,
and the stirring of the pots.

By Madhu Chitrakara.

271 Santal Pat (section)
Baramasia, Pakaur, Santal Parganas, Bihar
Earth colours on paper; 1'¾" x 11"
ca. 1930
Mildred and W. G. Archer Collection #202

Identified to a Santal audience as:
Sing Bonga (Chando Bonga, the Creator,
with white face), Jaher Era, the Lady
of the Sacred Grove and Marang Buru, the
Preserver (with blue face).*

By Girish Jadupatua.

*According to W. G. Archer.

272 Santal Pat (section)
Jamtara, Santal Parganas, Bihar
Earth colours on paper; 1'5¼" x 11"
ca. 1930
Mildred and W. G. Archer Collection #326

From a Krishna Lila Pat (scenes from
the life of Krishna).

273 Santal Pat (section)
From the same pat as no. 272. 1'5¼" x 11"
Mildred and W. G. Archer Collection #329

274 Santal Pat (section)
Ranga, Rajmahal, Santal Parganas, Bihar
Earth colours on paper; 1'5¼" x 11"
ca. 1930
Mildred and W. G. Archer Collection #174

Scenes from the life of Krishna:

1. Krishna flanked by two Gopinis fanning
him.

2. Krishna on his mother's lap; two
cowherds facing him.

By Babulal and Surendra Chitrakara.

275 Santal Pat (section)
From the same pat as no. 274.
Earth colours on paper; 2'10" x 11"
ca. 1930
Mildred and W. G. Archer Collection #178

Krishna, carrying curds, ferrying the
milkmaids across the Yamuna;
Radha-Krishna in a lotus-medallion. The
Rasa Lila dance of Krishna with the
Gopinis, projected into another lotus
medallion. Aquatic animals.

W. G. Archer gives the Santal explanation
of the two Hindu themes in the lotus:
the two standing figures being the first
Santal man and woman inside a "Kesalab"
stone under the water; the circular dance
represents the Creator, Chando Bonga,
holding a meeting.

276 Santal Pat (section)
From the same pat as nos. 274-275.
Earth colours on paper; 1'4½" x 11"
ca. 1930
Mildred and W. G. Archer Collection #179

a. Krishna milking while Yashoda holds
the cow.

b. The cowherds see Krishna as Vishnu.

Santal interpretation according to
W. G. Archer:

a. The first Santal man milks the cow, the
first Santal woman gives salt to the cow.

b. Chando Bonga, the Creator, with
two legendary Santals praying to him to
restore their names.

277 Santal Pat (section)
Bora, Dumka, Santal Parganas, Bihar
Earth colours on paper; 1'5" x 11"
ca. 1940
Mildred and W. G. Archer Collection #276

A story of the Santals. The scenes shown
here are Indra Daman Raja worshipping
Sengel Bonga, the four-headed one;
the eighteen heads of his sons.
A Santal dance, below.

By Praneshvar Chitrakara who explained
to W. G. Archer that Indra Daman Raja
went to Sengel Bonga, saying that he
had eighteen sons whom he could not
maintain. He asked if they could be beheaded
and turned into streams. Sengel Bonga
agreed and eighteen streams formed from
the blood which flowed from their heads.
This is why eighteen streams have to
be crossed in going to the Temple of
Jagannatha in Puri.

278 Santal Pat (section)
Bora, Dumka, Santal Parganas, Bihar
Market-bought colours on paper; 1'1½" x 11"
ca. 1940
Mildred and W. G. Archer Collection #279

Radha-Krishna and two milkmaids.

By Kirtan Chitrakara.

279 Santal Pat (section)
From the same scroll as no. 278.
Market-bought colours on paper; 1'5¼" x 11"
ca. 1940
Mildred and W. G. Archer Collection #282

Krishna in the branches of his Kadamba
tree having stolen the garments of
the cow-herdesses.

By Kirtan Chitrakara.

280 Kantha
Darbhanga, Bihar
Cotton embroidered cotton quilt; 6'6" x 3'11"
Early 20th century
Crafts Museum, New Delhi #M/7/2396

Widely spaced design on white ground,
emphasizing outlines. The interior tightly
filling stitches do or do not run parallel
to them. Kanthas from Bihar differ essentially
from those made in Bengal (East
Pakistan), nos. 414-445.

281 Kantha
Darbhanga, North Bihar
Cotton embroidered cotton quilt; 6'1" x 3'9"
Early 20th century
Crafts Museum, New Delhi #M/7/2398

282 Kantha
Darbhanga, North Bihar
Cotton embroidered cotton quilt;
6'2½" x 4'2⅞"
Early 20th century
Haku Shah, Ahmedabad

283 Chhau (Mask) of Shiva
Seraikella, Bihar
Painted over a compound of clay, paper,
and muslin cloth; 1'7¾" x 10¼" x 9½"
20th century
Asutosh Museum of Indian Art,
University of Calcutta #F.191

The serpent rearing above the head,
the Dhatura flower earrings, and the
third eye denote this mask as one of Shiva.

B. Orissa (nos. 284-315)

284 Krishna Dancing
Orissa
Copper; 8½" x 5" x 5"
17th century
Anonymous

The child Krishna, holding aloft two
butter balls (stolen from his mother),
dances in Chatura pose on a lotus pedestal.

285 Navagunjara
Plate XIX
Orissa
Brass; 8⅛" x 7⅞"
ca. 19th century
Nalini and Haridas K. Swali

With the head of a peacock, the body
of a tiger and the hump of a camel, one

leg of an elephant, the other of a horse, the tail being a snake, Lord Krishna in this disguise, holding in one hand which is that of a girl, a flower, appears before Arjuna testing his devotee whether he would recognise him. Arjuna immediately folds his hands and sings a song in praise of Lord Krishna who dances with joy in this assumed shape.

286 Gajalakshmi
Orissa
Brass; 7″ x 5″
ca. 17th-18th century
Mrs. Pupul Jayakar, New Delhi

The goddess "Luck," bathed by two elephants, is given here an outstandingly elegant image in the wire-technique of the lost wax process. Her two upper **hands** upholding the elephants form bridges within the circular opening which is part of her halo. The wire-technique encases her body with modelling power and lays a broad jewel collar on her shoulders which relates to the halo whose series of spiral discs fan out in the plane, proffering the pointed mystery of her delicately structured face. The legs crossed in Kurma Asana are shrunk to an indicative minimum, a feature not unusual in tribal Indian figurines. The pedestal, a rectangular stool, adds three-dimensional support by its boxlike seat.

287 Deity Seated
Kutiya Kond Tribe, Orissa – Andhra Pradesh border
Brass; 2½″ x 1⅞″
20th century
Victoria and Albert Museum, London
#I.S.55-1955

Flat body, loop-shaped legs on a bedlike stand.

288 Horse and Rider
Kutiya Kond Tribe, Orissa – Andhra Pradesh border
Brass; 6½″ x 5¾″
19th century
Victoria and Albert Museum, London
#I.M.117-1916

Cf. E. Thurston. *Castes and Tribes of South India*, pp. 388-91f.

289 Horse and Rider
Kutiya Kond Tribe, Orissa – Andhra Pradesh border
Brass; 7″ x 7″
20th century
Victoria and Albert Museum, London
#I.S.71-1955

290 Man Riding an Elephant
Kutiya Kond Tribe, Orissa – Andhra border
Brass; 6″ x 5″
20th century
Victoria and Albert Museum, London
#I.S.36-1955

291 Warrior
Plate XXIV
Kutiya Kond Tribe, Orissa – Andhra Pradesh border
Brass; 7⅛″ x 2¾″ x 2″
19th century
Victoria and Albert Museum, London
#I.M.118-1916

The warrior, his hair arranged in a top knot and wearing an upturned moustache, carries a battle-axe on his right shoulder, a hooked instrument in his left hand. Body of wire-lattice work; a length of cotton braid is arranged as a loincloth round his middle.

292 Female Figure
Plate XXIV
Kutiya Kond Tribe, Orissa – Andhra Pradesh border
Brass; 7⅛″ x 2¾″ x 2″
19th century
Victoria and Albert Museum, London
#I.M.119-1916

Cf. *Journal of Indian Art and Industry* (April, 1891), p. 10, Plate 30.

293 Jagannatha, "Lord of the World"
Puri, Orissa
Painted cloth over wood, sculpture in the round; 1′8⅗″ x 1′2″ x 6⅖″
ca. 1930
Dr. O. W. Samson, London

294 Jagannatha, Subhadra and Balarama
Puri, Orissa
Painted wood sculpture; 9½″ x 1′2¾″ x 4¾″
20th century
D. P. Ghosh, Calcutta

Subhadra is here assimilated in size to her brothers.

295 Mother and Child (Toy)
Orissa
Varnished and painted wood; 7½″ x 2¼″
20th century
Crafts Museum, New Delhi #M/5/80 (11)

296 Two Figures Embracing (Toy)
Orissa
Varnished and painted wood; 6½″ x 2″
20th century
Crafts Museum, New Delhi #M/5/80

297 Two Figures Embracing (Toy)
Orissa
Varnished and painted wood; 6¼″ x 2⅕″
20th century
Crafts Museum, New Delhi #16/112 (2)

298 Rama and Sita Enthroned
Orissa
Painting on palm leaves; 2′7″ x 1′½″
18th century
Poonam Backliwal, New Delhi

Seated under a double canopy, in the presence of Brahma, and accompanied by attendants, musicians and a dancer. The painting extends over several palm leaves strung together.

299 The Shakti Tower
Orissa
Painting on palm leaves; 1′10″ x 11¾″
18th century
Poonam Backliwal, New Delhi

Kama and Rati enthroned rest on the arms of two women acrobats, floating horizontally amongst an array of women acrobat-dancers forming a temple-tower-like pyramid in which the deities are ensconced. Flags, standards and fluttering garments enliven this configuration.

300 Jagannatha, Balabhadra and the Milkmaid Manika
Puri, Orissa
Varnished gouache painting on paper; 9½″ x 11″
18th century
Mildred and W. G. Archer Collection #49

Purushottama Deva, Raja of Orissa, when defeated by the Raja of Conjeeveram appealed to Jagannatha for help. The god promised to lead a counter expedition in person. On the way to join the god, the Raja of Orissa became nervous and longed for a sign. At that moment a milkmaid named Manika arrived and showed him a ring which she said had been given to her by two horsemen, one on a white horse and one on a black. Both horsemen were riding towards the enemy. The Raja of Orissa interpreted this as a sign that the gods were indeed coming to his help. He called the village where he halted, Manikapatana, the town of Manika. A wall painting of this subject is in the temple dancing hall.*

The interchange of colours, the white horse and the black-faced Jagannatha, the black horse of his elder brother Balabhadra (Balarama) whose face is white, is symbolic as well as decorative. Manika with a pot of curds on her head faces the riders.

*Note by W. G. Archer.

301 The Temple of Jagannatha
Puri, Orissa
Varnished gouache on cloth; 11″ x 9½″
18th century
Mildred and W. G. Archer Collection #64

The speckled ground of the painting is enriched by a Torana-like band on top showing the ten incarnations of Vishnu, Jagannatha standing for that of the Buddha. Shiva and Brahma on either side of the temple salute the enshrined trinity

(Jagannatha, Subhadra and Balarama). Three priests in front of the altar of the trinity. Below, two lions between them, and once more, Jagannatha, marking the entrance of his temple. The fish on the right represents the temple pond. Ritual objects and devotees, each in a little "niche," in a freely flowing symmetrical arrangement.

302 The Car of Jagannatha, Subhadra and Balarama Preceded by a Stag and Its Rider

Puri, Orissa
Varnished gouache on cloth; 8½″ x 10¾″
ca. 18th century
Mildred and W. G. Archer Collection #46

This painting is one of a group of six pictures, each showing a different outrider, i.e., horse, elephant, bullock, lion, Hanuman and a yellow stag. Although the exact significance of these emblematic outriders is uncertain, they may show the particular power which announces the presence of deity.

303 Vishnu Reclining on Ananta (Anantashayin)

Puri, Orissa
Varnished gouache on cloth; 4″ x 4⅝″
18th century
Anonymous

Vishnu resting in yoga-slumber on the world-serpent Ananta is shown here reclining in a half-sitting position on a coil of the seven-headed hissing serpent. Shri Devi and Bhu Devi, his consorts, holding lotuses, also seated on the serpent's body, face Vishnu. The three figures are in profile and are four armed. A small figure, Brahma, is seated back of the hoods of the serpent, on its tail. Colours: Indian red, ochre and indigo blue.

304 Jagannatha, Balabhadra and the Milkmaid Manika

Puri, Orissa
Varnished gouache on paper; 9″ x 11″
Early 19th century
Mildred and W. G. Archer Collection #50

Cf. no. 300. Here Manika greets the riders with folded hands. Two peacock feathers at the bottom stabilize the composition.

305 Krishna Playing the Flute, on a Boat, Accompanied by Another Boat

Puri, Orissa
Varnished gouache on paper; 9¾″ x 1′¼″
Early 19th century
Mildred and W. G. Archer Collection #53

The picture probably depicts the Chandana Jatra, a celebration held in April to May where a Krishna image and four lingas are taken daily on two boats to a small island in a pond with a temple in the centre.* In the painting, Krishna in his boat is followed by a boat with two dancers. The temple shapes on each boat suggest lingas.

*From a note by W. G. Archer.

306 The Temple of Jagannatha

Puri, Orissa
Varnished gouache on paper; 8¾″ x 10½″
Early 19th century
Mildred and W. G. Archer Collection #59

The trinity of the two brothers Jagannatha and Balarama and their sister Subhadra fills the temple. Its shape is reminiscent of the early shape of an Orissan Shikhara (temple tower). Six lamps on either side of the temple. Face and arms of each of the two brothers, together with their "body," make a trident shape.

307 The Temple of Jagannatha

Puri, Orissa
Varnished gouache on cloth; 4′9⅞″ x 3′5″
2nd quarter 20th century
Asutosh Museum of Indian Art, University of Calcutta #T.307

Cf. nos. 301 and 306.
Elaboration and schematization of the composition. The temple rises above a triple terrace, its high spire partly overlapped by the roof of the temple hall. In front of this, the trinity is part of a rectangular iconostasis with Shiva and Brahma flanking a Garuda-pillar. Door guardians on either side of this stepped structure, the whole being surrounded by the "air space." Horizontal rows with scenes from the life of Krishna, the worship of Jagannatha, etc. On top left, the Manika story (nos. 300, 304).

308 Jagannatha and Balarama Rigged Out for War

Puri, Orissa
Gouache on cloth; 2′5⅔″ x 2′8⅓″
Mid-20th century
Asutosh Museum of Indian Art, University of Calcutta #T.2339

Cf. the story of Manika, no. 300.
Priests and offerings. Shiva, Brahma, a nobleman and priests in rows at bottom.

309 A Musician

Puri, Orissa
Gouache on paper; 1′11″ x 1′5″
Mid-20th century
Asutosh Museum of Indian Art, University of Calcutta #T.311

310 The Story of Manika

Puri, Orissa
Varnished gouache on cloth; 1′¼″ x 1′7¼″
Beginning of 3rd quarter 20th century
Anonymous

Cf. no. 300. The horses, following the concept of Navanari-Kunjara, i.e., a horse made up of nine women, are here built up of three women, the women being Shakti or energy, carrying the gods into action. The opulent, unclothed, bejewelled figures are the main concern of the painter who is not ignorant of academic drawing. He translates it into fluid Orissan form without however the inner drive peculiar to this tradition of painting in the 18th century.

311 Two Horses Made of Four Women Each

Puri, Orissa
Beginning of 3rd quarter 20th century
Unvarnished gouache on cloth; 1′6¼″ x 1′
Anonymous

By the same hand as no. 310. An exercise in friezelike composition without reference to any particular legend but using a traditional concept for pictorial ends—into which the naturalistic and at the same time stylized treatment of the necks of the horses is made to blend.

312 Chira-Harana

Puri, Orissa
Unvarnished gouache on paper; 1′4¾″ x 1′7¾″
Beginning of 3rd quarter 20th century
Anonymous

Krishna having stolen the clothes of the milkmaids while they are bathing, plays on his flute, seated in the Kadamba tree.

313 Two-Headed Spotted Deer

Puri, Orissa
Varnished gouache on cloth; diam: 10⅙″
2nd quarter 20th century
Anonymous

314 Navagunjara

Puri, Orissa
Gouache on cloth; 10¼″ x 1′
2nd quarter 20th century
Anonymous

Navagunjara holds the conch of Vishnu of whom he is an avatar—his left hand is that of a woman as shown by the bangles on the arm and the short sleeve. Arjuna kneels facing Navagunjara whose camel's hump is marked with the trident of Shiva. Cf. no. 285.

315 Two-Headed Peacock

Puri, Orissa
Gouache on cloth; diam: 9¾″
2nd quarter 20th century
Anonymous

In each beak of his uncrested heads the peacock carries an elephant.

C. Bengal (West Bengal and East Pakistan) (nos. 316-445)

---

316 Krishna Venugopala

Bengal
Brass; 8½″ x 3¼″ x 2¾″
17th-18th century
Anonymous

Krishna, the cowherd, playing on a flute.

317

317 Simhasana
Bengal
Brass; 1′4″ x 10½″ x 6½″
18th-19th century
Anonymous

Stand, implicating a fantastic lion shape,
for a Shalagrama stone. (A Shalagrama stone
is a fossilized ammonite, a black ovoid
shape. It is a symbol of Vishnu.)

318 Durga
Bengal
Brass; 5″ x 3″ x 1¾″
18th century
Vittorio Cacciandra, Milan

The figure of the four-armed goddess riding
on her lion is connected by thin "wires" with
the delicate pillars upholding the high,
five-lobed arch of the stele.

319 Lakshmi
Bengal
Brass; 4½″ x 2¼″ x 2″
19th century
Anonymous

The crowned goddess standing with legs
crossed on a circular pedestal holds in
her left a lotus bud on a long stalk and in her
right a lotus pod on a long stalk, symbols
of the life cycle of the lotus whose
anthropomorphic image she is.

320 Gajalakshmi
Bengal
Brass; h: 7″
19th-20th century
Vittorio Cacciandra, Bombay

Standing image. Cf. no. 286 where the
goddess is seated.

321 Owl
Rampur, West Bengal
Brass; 3⅜″ x 2¾″ x 2¼″
20th century
Anonymous

322 Owl
Rampur, West Bengal
Brass; 3⅜″ x 2″ x 1¾″
20th century
Anonymous

323 Mukh-Dibba
Vishnupur, West Bengal
Brass; 1⅛″ x 2½″ x 1½″
18th to early 19th century
Anonymous

"Face casket" for serving "pan."

The subject could have been suggested
by the miniature face masks worn as magic
ornaments by the Konyak Naga.
Cf. no. 461.

324 Mukh-Dibba
Vishnupur, West Bengal
Brass; 3½″ x 4¾″ x 3½″
19th century
Anonymous

"Face casket" for serving "pan."

325 Asha Danda
Plate XLVIII
Sundarban, West Bengal
Brass; 8″ x 5¼″
20th century
Published: G. S. Dutt, "Tiger's God in Bengal
Art," *Modern Review* (1932), p. 522.
Anonymous

The double axe-shaped symbol of Lakshmi,
the goddess Fortune, represents the hope
(asha) of the Ghazi, a Moslem religious
mendicant who carries the staff (danda)
topped by this symbol to Hindu houses in
the morning during the Vrata celebration in
the month of Magh (January-February),
chanting that the goddess will give a boon
to those who perform the rites—including
the honouring of the Ghazi by a gift.

The tiger-god of Eastern India holds
as his symbols a rosary and an Asha Danda.

The symbol of the double axe appears
in Harappan art of ca. the 3rd millennium
B.C. on seals and painted pottery; cf. N. G.
Mazumdar, "Explorations in Sind," *Memoir,*
Archaeological Survey of India,
Plate 17, no. 38; Plate 15, no. 26; E. J. H.
Mackay, *Further Excavations at
Mohenjo-daro,* Plate 48, no. 12.

326 Krishna
Calcutta, West Bengal
Black stone; 1′8″ x 9″ x 9″
ca. 1920
Philadelphia Museum of Art, Philadelphia
#66-122-1

White and red paint on face, hands and feet.

**327 Carved Pilaster from a
Processional Car of Jagannatha**
Plates XXVI, XXVII
Moisadal, West Bengal
Wood; 7′ x 6″ x 1′
Early 19th century
Victoria and Albert Museum, London
#I.S.32-1956

The pilaster is carved on three of its faces
with armed figures, most of them riding on
elephants, lions and horses, and holding
spears and lances. The elephant rider at the
bottom of the pilaster, above its plain base,
thrusts his lance into a Makara, the great
monster of the deep. The action begins
beneath the plain capital where a male figure
on foot, naked but armed with swords,
steps forward. All the riders except the first
wear Western (Portuguese?) costume.
The subject represented on the pilasters,
of which there were four originally, is said to
represent the war of the demons Shumbha
and Nishumbha against the gods. The animals

in profile, the riders facing frontwards from above their seats, form an isocephalic relief on either side of the pilaster. Its projected middle part facing toward the front is transformed into a three-dimensional sequence of animal heads and riders' busts, in an outburst of animal energy and plastic power. Similar conceptions function as corner profiles on some of the carved brick temples of Bengal. (G. S. Dutt, "Bengali Terra-cottas," *Journal of the Indian Society of Oriental Art.* VI [1938], Plate 44.)

A terra-cotta incense burner from Tel Taanach, Israel, of the 11th century B.C., now in the Archaeological Museum at Istanbul, shows superimposed lions and sphinxes, the bodies in low relief, on the sides, the heads three-dimensional, forming the front corners.

328 Carved Pilaster from a Processional Car of Jagannatha

Plates XXVI, XXVII
Moisadal, West Bengal
Wood; 7' x 6" x 1'
Mid-19th century
Victoria and Albert Museum, London
#I.S.33.1956

This pilaster appears to be several decades later than no. 327. Substitution of female for male figures at the top of the pilaster where the rider on the lion represents the goddess Durga on her lion mount. She is shown large and naked, holding swords. Bulls, without riders, are interpolated between the other animals. Schematized western naturalism of modelling and wilder commotion of figures than in no. 327.

329 Carved Lintel

Birbhum, West Bengal
Wood; 1'5" x 4' x 3"
ca. 1800
Bengal Bratachari Society, Calcutta
#GM/1342

Framed by a fillet carved in low relief with interlacing waves enclosing lotus rosettes, the panel shows: Durga killing the buffalo demon, Lakshmi, Sarasvati, Karttikeya and Ganesha, two attendant goddesses on lotus flowers, and two small naked female figures, squatting with their legs drawn up, the arms brought forward from below their knees, the hands in Anjali Mudra (salutation), and an acrobat on a peg in the extreme left, on a ground with lotuses and palmettes in low relief.

330 Crouching Woman

Comilla, East Bengal, East Pakistan
Polychromed wood, sculpture in the round; 1'2" x 11" x 9"
Early 19th century
Bengal Bratachari Society, Calcutta
#GM/1304

331A, B Two Owls

A Natungram, Burdwan, West Bengal
B West Bengal
Wood, painted and varnished; 10⅛" x 5"; 9¼" x 5", respectively
1st half 20th century
Crafts Museum, New Delhi #M/7/2354

332A, B, C Vrishakashtha

Natun Bazar, Calcutta, West Bengal
Wood, painted,
A and C: 6'6¾" x 3⅝" x 1¼"
B: 6'10¾" x 3⅝" x 1¼"
1966
Philadelphia Museum of Art, Philadelphia
#67-197-7

Three "bull-posts" or Vrishakashtha. A Vrishakashtha is set up for one year after a death. From the top: The spire of a Bengal temple and a trident of Shiva, instead of a linga, enshrined; a bull enshrined; the face of the dead, the hand holding a rosary, the plain, long and thin post, and, below, much further down, the feet.

The work of an aged woman, widow of a woodcarver.

333 Doll

Natungram, Burdwan, West Bengal
Painted wood; 7¼" x 2"
2nd quarter 20th century
Asutosh Museum of Indian Art, University of Calcutta #T.720

A vertical slab of wood, half cylindrical in front, the back flat, represents a female figure. Head and neck are carved; painted summarily red, black, white and yellow in large planes organized by bold brush strokes. Nos. 333-341 are of the wood-slab type, a basic shape of Bengali dolls.

334 Doll

Serampur, Hooghly, West Bengal
Wood, painted and varnished; 8½" x 2½"
ca. 1939
Mildred and W. G. Archer collection #20

Female figure.

335 Doll

Vishnupur, Bankura, West Bengal
Painted and varnished wood; 9½" x 2"
20th century
Asutosh Museum of Indian Art, University of Calcutta #F.5

Female figure.

336 Doll

Dacca, East Pakistan
Painted and varnished wood; 9½" x 2½"
20th century
Published: M. K. Pal, *Catalogue of the Asutosh Museum* (Calcutta University, 1962), p. 23, Fig. 27, Plate 12.
Asutosh Museum of Indian Art, University of Calcutta #4

Figure of a man with a moustache, the

334

body blocked out from the wooden slab,
the painting descriptive of pattern and folds
of a regal costume. The figure is said
to represent Lakshmana.

337 Doll
Bengal
Painted and varnished wood; 7⅖″ x 2½″
20th century
Crafts Museum, New Delhi #M/4/357 (2)

338 Doll
Kalighat, Bengal
Painted and varnished wood; 6½″ x 2″
20th century
Crafts Museum, New Delhi #M/4/357 (1)

339 Doll
Bengal
Painted and varnished wood; 8½″ x 2⅔″
20th century
Crafts Museum, New Delhi #M/16/100 (2)

340 Doll
Kalighat, Bengal
Painted and varnished wood; 6½″ x 1⅕″
20th century
Crafts Museum, New Delhi #5/79

341 Doll
Bengal
Painted and varnished wood; 7″ x 1¾″
20th century
Crafts Museum, New Delhi #4.153 (1)

342 Gauranga (Toy)
Navadvip, West Bengal
Carved and painted wood; 7⅛″ x 5½″
20th century
Asutosh Museum of Indian Art,
University of Calcutta #T.1872

Gauranga is a surname of Chaitanya
(1485-1536), the ecstatic visionary and
devotee of Krishna. Influence of "naturalism"
and of figurines modelled in clay.

343 Circular Mould for Mango Paste
Jessore, East Pakistan
Carved stone; diam: 10″
20th century
Bengal Bratachari Society, Calcutta #GM/14

Krishna, shown twice, symmetrically in
three-branched Kadamba tree. Below:
Gopinis, nude to the hips and wearing
long skirts; the entire roundel down to the
triangular roots of the tree filled with
Kadamba flower rosettes.

344 Circular Mould for Mango Paste
Jessore, East Pakistan
Carved stone; diam: 11″
Early 20th century
Bengal Bratachari Society, Calcutta #GM/10

Peacock in center, two human figures,
bird and floral border.

345 Mould for Mango Paste
Bengal
Stone; width: 6″
Early 20th century
Asutosh Museum of Indian Art,
University of Calcutta #T.7100

346 Rama
West Bengal
Carved brick; 7⅛″ x 5¼″ x 2″
ca. 17th century
Philadelphia Museum of Art, Philadelphia
#66-189-9

Rama standing in vehement Alidha, or
archer's posture, on the Makara of his chariot.

347 Dancer
West Bengal
Carved brick; 5″ x 3½″ x 1½″
ca. 17th century
Anonymous

348 Krishna and Two Gopinis
Bengal
Carved brick; 6⅝″ x 5⁵⁄₁₆″ x 1¼″
18th century
Philadelphia Museum of Art, Philadelphia
#66-189-11

Figures in cusped niche, scrollwork above.

349 Krishna and Cows
West Bengal
Carved brick; 4¾″ x 6¼″ x 2″
19th century
Philadelphia Museum of Art, Philadelphia
#66-189-10

Krishna seated, playing the flute under two
Kadamba trees; two cows raise their
heads toward him.

**350 Man with Two Hunting Dogs
and a Bird Having a Human Head**
Mathurapur, West Bengal
Carved brick; 7¼″ x 6″
19th century
Bengal Bratachari Society, Calcutta
#GM/679

351 Deer in Flight
Mathurapur, West Bengal
Carved brick; 7¼″ x 6″
19th century
Bengal Bratachari Society, Calcutta
#GM/677

Cf. G. S. Dutt, "Bengali Terra-cottas,"
*Journal of the Indian Society of Oriental
Art,* VI (1938), 169-80, Plates 38, 39.

352 Two Lions Having Human Heads
Jessore, East Pakistan
Carved brick; 7″ x 6″
19th century
Published: G. S. Dutt, *Journal of the
Indian Society of Oriental Art,*
Vol. VI (1938).
Bengal Bratachari Society, Calcutta
#GM/675

343
―――
346
―――
349

353
356

353 Manasa Ghat
Barisal, East Pakistan
Painting on terra-cotta; 1'1⁄4" x 71⁄2"
20th century
Asutosh Museum of Indian Art,
University of Calcutta #F.756

The serpent-goddess Manasa is one with
the pot (ghat) in which she is worshipped.
Behind her serpent crown emerges a
small figure in profile with flowing hair.

Cf. E. C. Dimock, Jr., "The Goddess of
Snakes in Mediaeval Bengali Literature,"
History of Religions, I (Chicago, 1962),
307-21.

354 Manasa Ghat
Bankura, West Bengal
Black terra-cotta; 1'1⁄4" x 71⁄2"
20th century
Asutosh Museum of Indian Art,
University of Calcutta #F.830

355 Mother and Child
Hooghly, West Bengal
Lacquered terra-cotta; 41⁄2" x 31⁄2"
2nd half 20th century
Asutosh Museum of Indian Art,
University of Calcutta #F.798

Basic shapes of cone or cylinder make
up this group.

356 Male Figurine
Murshidabad, West Bengal
Painted terra-cotta; 4" x 21⁄2"
1944
Victoria and Albert Museum, London
#I.S.104-1952

Basic shape.

357 Mother and Child
Keto, Murshidabad, West Bengal
Painted terra-cotta; 63⁄4" x 31⁄2"
2nd quarter 20th century
Asutosh Museum of Indian Art,
University of Calcutta #T.1515

Face moulded "naturalistically" on
basic shape of figurine.

358 Equestrian Figurine
Keto, Murshidabad, West Bengal
Painted terra-cotta; 71⁄2" x 51⁄4" x 31⁄2"
2nd quarter 20th century
Published: *Catalogue of Folk Art, op. cit.,*
p. 27, Plate 15.1.
Asutosh Museum of Indian Art,
University of Calcutta #T.1513

Hand modelled, basic shapes, face
moulded. Painted red, ivory and black on
mica-dusted, silvery ground.

359 Elephant (Toy)
Astagram, Chittagong, East Pakistan
Painted terra-cotta; 41⁄2" x 41⁄2" x 21⁄4"
20th century
Asutosh Museum of Indian Art,
University of Calcutta #F.665B

Painted varicoloured stripes are
characteristic of Bengali clay figurines.

360 Equestrian Figurine (Toy)
Astagram, Chittagong, East Pakistan
Painted terra-cotta; 43⁄4" x 51⁄8" x 31⁄8"
20th century
Asutosh Museum of Indian Art,
University of Calcutta #F.665A

361 Deer (Toy)
Astagram, Chittagong, East Pakistan
Painted terra-cotta; 51⁄2" x 41⁄2" x 23⁄4"
20th century
Asutosh Museum of Indian Art,
University of Calcutta #F.664A

362 Two Horses (Toys)
Andal, Burdwan, West Bengal
Painted cloth over straw, etc.;
8" x 43⁄4" x 31⁄4", each
20th century
Published: *Catalogue of Folk Art, op. cit.,*
p. 27, Plate 15.3.
Asutosh Museum of Indian Art,
University of Calcutta #T.1824, A and B

Black horses with paper appliqué in
contrasting colours on cloth over cord
and stuffing of straw, jute and sand.

363 Horse of the Gajan Dancers
Burartat, Sundarban, West Bengal
Bamboo, cloth, paper and jute;
4'11" x 1'113⁄4" x 71⁄4"
20th century
Asutosh Museum of Indian Art,
University of Calcutta #F.823

364 The Swoon of Chaitanya
Bankura, West Bengal
Painting on wood; 51⁄4" x 1'3⁄4"
ca. 1800
Asutosh Museum of Indian Art,
University of Calcutta #19

One of a pair of painted wooden covers
of a manuscript.

365 Woman and Child
Calcutta
Watercolour painting on handmade paper;
93⁄4" x 71⁄16"
Early 19th century
Robert M. Shapazian, Fresno, California

Indian version, corresponding to
contemporary fashion plates such as
appeared in *Costume of Hindostan*
by Balt, Solvyns, of Calcutta, London, 1804.

366 Krishna Lila Pat
Murshidabad, West Bengal
Scroll painting, gouache on paper; 6'3" x 1'2"
ca. 1800
Victoria and Albert Museum, London
#I.S.106-1955

The vertical scroll (pat) depicts a local
version of the story of the birth of Krishna
according to the Bhagavata Purana. The
tyrant-king Kansa knew that a child born to
Devaki would destroy him. He ordered
that any child born to her should be slain.

Measures are taken by Devaki and Vasudeva
to save their children as soon as born.
In vain. Finally, the eighth child, to be
born, was Krishna, incarnation of God
(Narayana) who was to save the world
from the tyrant. The painting illustrates
events preceding the birth of Krishna:

a. Pregnant Devaki is taken in a palanquin
at night from her house to an island
considered a safe place for her delivery.
The party is escorted by an officer of
Vasudeva and is followed by their dog.

b. Devaki lying on a cot guarded by snakes
and tigers on the island.

c. Two of the palanquin bearers treacherously
inform Kansa about Devaki's flight;
a courtier advises Kansa to take
immediate action.

d. Mother and child rest, guarded by
snakes and tigers.

e. An officer of King Kansa arrives at
Vasudeva's house, a doorkeeper implores
him to have mercy and keep the matter
secret. In vain. Vasudeva is put in prison.
(The child, it is to be inferred, was killed.)

f. Incensed Brahmans beat the cruel
officer of Kansa.

g. Brahman astrologers predict that the Lord
(Narayana) is to be born as son of Vasudeva
and as a saviour in the house of Nanda.
Vasudeva is given the tidings.

h. Nanda and the Brahmans invoke
Narayana. He manifests and they pray that
he incarnate to kill Kansa.

367A, B Ramayana Pat (two sections)
Plate XXXIII, (detail)
Hooghly, West Bengal
Gouache on paper; 1'5" x 1'8", each panel
Early 19th century
Published: A. Ghose, "Old Bengal Paintings,"
Rupam, Calcutta, 1926, pp. 27-28.
Anonymous

The painting on deep Indian red ground
sets off its widely spaced figures in ochre and
deep indigo blue, with sharp profiles of
their faces. The two panels illustrate
the story of the golden deer. In this disguise
Maricha, a demon, bewitched Sita by its
beauty. Coveting the golden deer, she
prevailed on Rama to leave their retreat in
pursuit of the deer. When Rama was about to
kill it, the deer revealed himself as the
demon sent by Ravana, the demon king, in
order to abduct Sita in the absence of
Rama and his brother Lakshmana.

Another though less powerfully painted
pat of this style is in the Asutosh Museum,
University of Calcutta (A. Mookerjee,
Folk Art of Bengal, Calcutta, 1939,
Plates 22, 23).

366 detail

368 Shakti Pat
Bankura, West Bengal
Scroll painting, gouache on paper;
9'8½" x 1'4½"
Early 20th century
Asutosh Museum of Indian Art,
University of Calcutta #T.7094

Painted in homage of the Great Goddess,
in her various forms of manifestation. At the
bottom of the scroll: Kali dancing on
the cremation ground, on the corpse of
Shiva whom, dancing, she awakens to life.

369 Santal Pat
Lohati, Bankura, West Bengal
Earth colours on paper; 15'7½" x 9"
2nd quarter 20th century
Asutosh Museum of Indian Art,
University of Calcutta #T.7093

Illustrating the origin of mankind according
to Santal myth: Vishnu created the
original man and woman. He married them;
they had six sons and six daughters. The
parents drank, quarrelled and separated.
Time passed. Once, in a forest, six young men
saw six girls swinging on trees. Without
recognising one another, they married
and the human race grew.

The Santal scrolls, whether painted in
Bengal or in Bihar, whether painted by
Chitrakaras or Jadu-Patuas form a distinct
style group when compared with other scroll
paintings from Bengal. Cf. nos. 265-279.

The subjects of a Santal scroll are either
Hindu, but often reinterpret Hindu themes
according to Santal tradition, or illustrations
of Santal themes.

370 Santal Portrait of the Dead
Bankura, West Bengal
Earth colours on paper; 10¼" x 9⅛"
ca. 2nd quarter 20th century
Anonymous

A man seated on a string bed with the
right leg raised and the right elbow resting
on it with the hand raised and turned
in the gesture of exposition (cinmudra).
Face in profile, body in three-quarter profile.
The left hand closed to a fist rests on
the left leg. An earthen pot and a plate, on
the right. The figure is clad in a white dhoti.

371 Santal Portrait of the Dead
Bankura, West Bengal
Earth colours on paper; 10¼" x 9⅛"
ca. 2nd quarter 20th century
Anonymous

A woman. The figure wears a white sari
of narrow width with a border. On the right
proper: a rosary hung on a peg, a
plate and tumbler.

372 Santal Portrait of the Dead
Bankura, West Bengal
Earth colours on paper; 10¼" x 9⅛"
ca. 2nd quarter 20th century
Anonymous

(Torn fragment). A young man.

380 detail
384 detail

373 Ramayana Pat
Katowa, Burdwan, West Bengal
Gouache on paper; 12′3¼″ x 1′9¾″
Late 19th century
Asutosh Museum of Indian Art,
University of Calcutta #T.2242

Episodes from the Ramayana, in murky
colours, conventional "Western" shading of
figures whose faces are generally in front view.

374 Krishna Lila Pat (Scroll Painting of the Life of Krishna) (part only)
Birbhum, West Bengal
Gouache on paper; 8′ x 1′8″
Late 19th century
Anonymous

The predominant colours are, on light
Indian red ground; rose, terre verte, plum
colour, white and deep blue. The
Sarpabandha, or serpent interlace with
Krishna in its midst* is an application of a
symbolic diagram, in a narrative context.
The serpent Yantra also figures amongst
diagrams drawn on the floor.

*This refers to Krishna subduing the
serpent Kaliya. Re: Sarpabandha incised
on stone pillars of the eleventh century, cf.
Archaeological Survey of India, Western Circle,
1918-19, p. 46, No. 10; 1912-13, p. 55, No. 5.

Cf. also Stella Kramrisch, "An Illuminated
Gita Govinda Manuscript," *Journal of
the Indian Society of Oriental Art,* II
(Calcutta), 119-21, Plate 29.

375 Vaishnava Pat
Birbhum, West Bengal
Scroll painting, gouache on paper;
7′1¾″ x 1′8¼″
Late 19th to early 20th century
Philadelphia Museum of Art, Philadelphia
#65-183-2

Part only; showing large figure of Krishna
at the end of the scroll. Above, the story
of the Naramedha Yajna—told in the
Aitareya Brahmana—of the human sacrifice
by King Nahusha, the purchase of the boy
from his old Brahman father, and the
rescue of the boy by Lord Narayana.

376A, B Shakti Pat
Birbhum, West Bengal
Scroll painting, gouache on paper;
20′2½″ x 1′6½″
19th century
Published (detail): *Journal of the Indian
Society of Oriental Art,* XIII, (1945),
Plate 12.
Philadelphia Museum of Art, Philadelphia
#64-169-4

377A, B Ramayana Pat
Birbhum, West Bengal
Gouache on paper; 13′9″ x 1′6½″
Late 19th century
#64-169-3 (a, b)

Episodes from the Ramayana, the bird
Jatayus with Ravana and Sita in his
beak being most prominent.

378 Santal Pat
Kenduli, Birbhum, West Bengal
Earth colours on paper; 4′9″ x 10¾″
Late 19th century
Asutosh Museum of Indian Art,
University of Calcutta #T.2936

A sequence of scenes showing an equestrian
figure, soldiers, a deer attacked by a hyena,
a deer attacked by a wolf, a canine
animal followed by birds.

379 The Legend of Kamala-Kamini
Midnapur, West Bengal
Scroll painting, gouache on paper;
11′10½″ x 1′7½″
20th century
Asutosh Museum of Indian Art,
University of Calcutta #T.2575

Detail on top: the fleet of the merchant
Chand Sadagar. The main scene shows the
miracle of the lotus-goddess seen by the
merchant in mid-ocean while she swallows
an elephant and again ejects him.

380A, B Krishna Lila Pat (Scroll Painting of the Life of Krishna)
Plate XXXII (detail)
Midnapur, West Bengal
Gouache on paper; 12′9½″ x 1′9″
19th century
Anonymous

The early life of Krishna is the subject
of this scroll. The single, miraculous events
follow, scene upon scene, along the blue
band of the river Jamuna where they played.
At the bottom, the scene of Krishna having
stolen the clothes of the cow-herdesses,
shows his small figure amidst the
foliage of the Kadamba tree whose stem
is crowned by the sun.

The ripples of the water of the river
reverberate in the curves of the folds of
the garments, its sinuosities in the shape of
the bodies and the way in which trees grow.
Dots and lines enliven areas coloured
rose, mauve, indigo and ochre, on a
white ground.

381 Ghazi Pat
Midnapur, West Bengal
Scroll painting, gouache on paper;
5′10½″ x 1′2¼″
Late 19th century
Asutosh Museum of Indian Art,
University of Calcutta #T.7649

Scrolls illustrating the cult of the tiger-god
address themselves to Hindus and Moslems
(cf. no. 265). They depict events in the
career of Barekhan Ghazi or Satya Pir,
the tiger-god and punishments met out by
his faithful tigers to those who refused to
offer oblations. The Ghazi carries a rosary
and an Asha Danda.

388

382 Ramayana Pat
Midnapur, West Bengal
Scroll painting, gouache on paper;
12′9″ x 1′7½″
Mid-19th century
Asutosh Museum of Indian Art,
University of Calcutta #T.2574

383 Rama Lila Pat
Tamluk, Midnapur, West Bengal
Scroll painting, gouache on paper;
19′4¼″ x 1′9″
Mid-19th century
Asutosh Museum of Indian Art,
University of Calcutta #7

Incidents from the story of Rama.

384 The Legend of Behula
Midnapur, West Bengal
Scroll painting, gouache on paper;
8′7½″ x 1′5¾″
Late 19th century
Asutosh Museum of Indian Art,
University of Calcutta #15

Behula, the devoted wife, accompanies
on a raft the corpse of her husband who
had died of snakebite on account of the wrath
of Manasa, the snake-goddess. When the
body reaches the domain of Manasa
she restores to life the decomposed corpse.
The image of Manasa is painted large
on the top of the scroll.

Re: the story of Behula, cf. D. C. Sen,
"Behula: A Myth of the Snake Goddess,"
Modern Review, Calcutta, 1907, pp. 26-35.

385 Jagannatha Pat
Manbhum, Purulia, West Bengal
Scroll painting, gouache on paper; 4′ x 2′¼″
ca. 1925
Philadelphia Museum of Art, Philadelphia
#64-169-2

Upper part only: Jagannatha, Subhadra
and Balarama enshrined in a temple of
Bengali architectural type; at the
bottom: Garuda, monkeys, etc. Painted on
discarded railway timetables, dated 1922.

386A, B The Legend of Behula
Manbhum, Purulia, West Bengal
Scroll painting, gouache on paper;
14′5¼″ x 1′5″
Early 20th century
Philadelphia Museum of Art, Philadelphia
#64-169-5(a,b)

Crudely and frontally shown, large
headed and large eyed figures cover the
ground. A wavy line across the chest
indicates its modelling. This is an ancient
Indian sculptural convention.

387A, B Naramedha Pat
Bandarpur, West Bengal
Gouache on paper; 22′2¼″ x 1′11½″
Dated 1916
Philadelphia Museum of Art, Philadelphia
#64-169-1(a,b)

The legend of Nahusha and Yajati
(cf. no. 375). For variety and liveliness
of local styles of the village painters
about half a century ago, cf. nos. 385, 386.

By Durlav Chitrakara.

388-413
Paintings and Brush Drawings from Kalighat,
West Bengal

---

388 Sarasvati
Kalighat
Watercolours and silver on paper; 1′2″ x 10″
ca. 1875
Anonymous

The goddess of knowledge, holding
a lute and seated on a lotus. The yellow
ground enhances the red, black, mauve and
green colours, heightened by silver lines
and dots and the flesh tint modelled in grey.

**389 Woman Holding Rose and
Peacock**
Kalighat
Watercolours and silver, on paper:
1′3¼″ x 10¼″
ca. 1870
Pramod Chandra, Chicago

390 Woman and Parrot
Plate XXXIV
Kalighat
Brush drawing on paper; 1′5¼″ x 10¼″
ca. 1875
Anonymous

391 Woman Holding a Rose
Kalighat
Brush drawing on paper; 1′5¼″ x 10¾″
ca. 1875
Published: Stella Kramrisch, *The Art of
India,* 1965, p. 124.
Anonymous

The balance of classical Indian (Yakshini)
with classical Western elements (sleeping
Ariadne) is seen in the raised arm
and in the treatment of the breasts, their
exaggeration being Indian, their being set
wide apart as in Greek sculpture,
contrary to the Indian ideal which brings
them close together so that they touch.

392 Jagaddhatri
Kalighat
Watercolours and silver on paper;
1′5⅞″ x 10¾″
1875-1880
Anonymous

In this form of hers the Great Goddess
rides on her lion who has overcome

an elephant; only the head of the elephant is shown. The paper is divided by pencil lines making a linear grid in which the composition is laid out. Corners cut off.

393 The Tarakeshvar Scandal (The Murder Trial)
Kalighat
Watercolours on paper; 1'4" x 11"
ca. 1875
Dr. O. W. Samson, London

The chief priest (mahant) of the temple at Tarakeshvar near Calcutta carried on an affair with Elokeshi, the wife of a young Brahman who worked in the office of the Superintendent of Government Printing, Calcutta. Having come to know of the intrigue he severed with a fish knife the head of his wife.

The main figures in the picture are: the English judge, the murdered Elokeshi with head off between the feet of the judge and his footstool, the chief priest with hands joined, behind bars; on the other side of Elokeshi is her husband.

Cf. W. G. Archer, *Bazaar Paintings,* Plate 7 and *Kalighat Drawings,* Bombay, 1962, pp. 11-13.

394 The Mahant of Tarakeshvar Fanning Elokeshi
Kalighat
Watercolours on paper; 1'6" x 11¼"
ca. 1875
Mildred and W. G. Archer Collection #26

Elokeshi sits on a chair and holds a rose. Illustration of the Tarakeshvar scandal of 1873.

395 Durga Simhavahini
Kalighat
Watercolours on paper and silver paint; 1'5½" x 11"
ca. 1880
Mildred and W. G. Archer Collection #32

The goddess on her lion trampling on the demon general Raktabija.

396 The Brinjal Plant
Kalighat
Watercolours on paper; 1'4" x 11"
End 19th century
Dr. O. W. Samson, London

A very large Brinjal (Aubergine) plant occupies the field. In the right corner an elegant little lady points to one of the fruits; a child holds a thread entwined round the stem of the fruit. This may illustrate the story of Princess Aubergine. A poor gardener asked a market gardener for alms. He gives him a Brinjal. A fairy princess comes out of the Brinjal fruit. (C. W. Crooke, "North Indian Notes and Queries, IV," *Indian Antiquary,* XXIII [London, 1894], 117.)

397 Kali
Kálighat
Watercolours on paper; 1'7" x 11"
End 19th century
Dr. O. W. Samson, London

Kali, a form of the Great Goddess, is the "power of time," the power of destruction of all existence. She gives release from existence.

398 Hanuman with Rama and Sita in His Heart
Kalighat
Watercolours on paper; 1'4" x 11"
Late 19th century
Dr. O. W. Samson, London

399-413, from Kalighat, are of the same period (end of the 19th to early 20th century) and size (1'5⅞" x 11⅛"). Anonymous.

399 Shiva Carrying the Dead Sati

400 Shiva Playing the Lute

401 Harihara

Deity whose right half is Shiva, the Creator and Destroyer, and whose left is Vishnu, the Preserver of the Universe.

402 Narasimha Avatar

The man-lion incarnation of Vishnu in which he kills the demon king "Gold-Cloth" (Hiranyakashipu)—who had challenged the omnipresence of Vishnu—by tearing his entrails.

403 Durga Killing the Demon Nishumbha

404 Krishna and Balarama

Krishna and Balarama under a tree, Balarama holding a calf. Both stand on lotus flowers.

405 Radha and Krishna

406 Yashoda Milking a Cow

The foster mother of Krishna; Krishna back of her.

407 Advaita and Nityananda

The foremost disciples of Chaitanya.

408 Shyamakanta Banerji Wrestling with a Tiger

Cf. W. G. Archer, *Kalighat Drawings, op. cit.,* p. 9.

409 Fish and Crayfish

410 Cat Holding a Fish in Its Mouth

411 Cat Holding a Crayfish in Its Mouth

412 Cat Holding a Parrot in Its Mouth

413 Red Parrot on Tree

414-445
Kanthas, multicoloured cotton embroideries on white, patched and quilted cotton cloth.

414 Kantha
Colour Plate XLII
Khulna, East Pakistan
Coloured cotton embroidery on white quilt; 2'8¾" x 2'7"
Early 19th century
Published: Stella Kramrisch, "Kanthas of Bengal," *Marg,* III, 1949, 20; "Textiles and Ornaments of India," *op. cit.,* p. 62 (detail).
Anonymous

The mandala design of this Kantha shows in the middle of each side twice two lotuses in a rectangular passage leading to the central square. The "modelling" of the female figures by a change of the direction and density of the stitches, the "transparency" of the horse with its rider, the real and phantastic animals, the linga-shrine, bird, fish, serpent symbols and many others elegantly fill the partitioned field.

415 Kantha
Khulna, East Pakistan
Cotton embroidered cotton patchwork quilt; 5'8" x 3'9¾"
Second half 19th century
Published: Stella Kramrisch, "Kantha," *Journal of the Indian Society of Oriental Art,* VII (1939), Plate 15, 3 (detail); *Marg,* III, 20, 25; *Textiles and Ornaments of India, op. cit.,* vii, frontispiece.
Anonymous

Peacocks fill the corners of the inner square around the central lotus. The broad border is subdivided into rectangular panels, each of which offers its decorated field, the compositions ranging from panels with floral symbolism to others based on the temple car, on animal symbols and on groups of dancers. Flat stitches and decorative use of many colours heighten the effect of this brilliant Kantha which also uses some otherwise rarely employed symbols like double triangles and double spirals each in its rhythmically appointed place, each adjusted in size and shape to the visual context of the whole.

415 detail

416 Kantha
Colour Plate xxxix (detail)
Khulna, East Pakistan
Cotton and silk embroidered cotton quilt;
7½" x 2'
Late 19th to early 20th century
Published: *Marg*, III (1949), l.c., pp. 22-23.
Anonymous

In this splendid, small, oblong Kantha,
coloured silk thread is used not only for
part of the figures but also for the ground.
Four women on one side of the central
lotus and three men on the other side perform
a harvest (?) dance. The movement
of body and drapery are enhanced by the
patterns of differently spaced stitches.
Whirls, waves, life tree, birds, and part of
a large lotus flower fill the ground.

417 Kantha
Khulna, East Pakistan
Cotton embroidered cotton patchwork; 2' x 6"
Early 20th century
Bengal Bratachari Society, Calcutta
#GM/1599

Three lotuses, Radha and Krishna; and
Durga killing the buffalo demon,
between them.

418 Kantha
Jessore, East Pakistan
Cotton embroidered cotton patchwork;
1'11" x 7¼"
19th century
Anonymous

Temple car and enshrined deities. Each
wheel moreover is surmounted by its deity
which is given a niche.

419 Kantha
Jessore, East Pakistan
Cotton embroidered cotton patchwork;
2'7" x 2'7"
19th century
Anonymous

Almost exclusively floral and geometrical.

420 Kantha
Jessore, East Pakistan
Cotton embroidered cotton patchwork;
2'9" x 9½"
19th century
Published: *Marg*, III (1949), 29.
Anonymous

The long strip is divided into two parts,
the design facing in opposite directions. The
one part shows a temple car having
six niches each filled by a figure; an elephant,
fish and whirls below; the other part
filled with animal and floral symbols.
Of special interest is the effect of closely
running parallel lines, one continuous, the
other dotted, and the accentuation
of the entire embroidered field by the
black dots of coiffures, symbols, etc.

418 detail

424 detail

.421 **Kantha**
Jessore, East Pakistan
Embroidered cotton quilt; 2'8½" x 2'11½"
ca. Mid-19th century
Published: *Journal of the Indian Society of Oriental Art*, l.c., Plate 12.
Anonymous.

The central "lotus" with its eight-pronged central star, surrounded by life tree, i.e. "Kalka" motifs, in various combinations, and a marginal border of evolution-involution scrolls. The corners are filled by life trees. Of the four main animals in the middle of each side, the great horse carries the sun, and the bull a Shiva-linga. A foppish Westerner sits on a kind of Empire chair. Birds, fish, whirls, creepers, ears of grain, etc., help to fill the ground.

422 **Kantha**
Jessore, East Pakistan
Embroidered cotton quilt; 3'6¾" x 1'9"
2nd half 19th century
Published: *Journal of the Indian Society of Oriental Art*, l.c., Plate 13, 2 (detail).
Anonymous

Birds pecking seeds from the central lotus-field, here stylized as a hexagonal leaf interlace; and life trees (kalka). The Kalka originated as a cypress tree in Persian design, thence transformed in the woolen Kashmir shawls it was assimilated in Bengal to the shape of a mango.

423 **Kantha**
Jessore, East Pakistan
Embroidered cotton quilt; 2'6" x 2'6½"
2nd half 19th century
Anonymous

Prominence of central lotus, surrounded by equestrian figures, animals, plants. Border of life trees.

424 **Kantha**
Jessore, East Pakistan
Embroidered cotton quilt; 6'1" x 4'2½"
Second half 19th century
Published: *Journal of the Indian Society of Oriental Art*, l.c., Plate 15.1 (detail).
Anonymous.

The design imitates the effect of a woven pattern. The maker of this Kantha belonged to the weaver caste. Whereas, in all the other types of Kanthas, front and back are almost the same, here a particular stitch is used which helps to cover the ground in front and hardly shows at the back.

425 **Kantha**
Jessore, East Pakistan
Embroidered cotton quilt; 2'8½" x 2'8¾"
Late 19th century
Published: *Journal of the Indian Society of Oriental Art*, l.c., Plate 13, 3.
Anonymous

The design, divided into four compartments around a central lotus and between

corner life trees shows:

a. Durga, her head surmounted by Shiva on Nandi; flanked by Ganesha, etc.

b. Ten heads riding on an elephant and a decapitated head.

c. A horseman.

d. A life tree and the following poem:

"Impermanent is mundane existence behold,
Impermanent the body; it does not stay,
The water on a lotus leaf.
Say Hari, say Hari,*
The name of Hari is Truth,
Mundane existence is impermanent,
This Kantha's owner:
Shri Harilal Kundu."

*Hari is the name of God (Vishnu).

The border imitates a woven "Kalka" design.

426 **Kantha**
Panjia, Jessore, East Pakistan
Embroidered cotton quilt; 6'6" x 3'10"
Late 19th century
Published: *Marg.*, III, l.c., Colourplate 8 (detail).
Anonymous

427 **Kantha**
Panjia, Jessore, East Bengal, East Pakistan
Embroidered cotton quilt; 2'2½" x 9½"
Late 19th century
Asutosh Museum of Indian Art, University of Calcutta #T.6577

Lotus-wave (Kalpalata).

428 **Kantha**
Jessore, East Pakistan
Embroidered cotton quilt; 6'3½" x 4'1"
Late 19th century
Published: *Journal of the Indian Society of Oriental Art*, l.c., Calcutta, 1939, Plate 11.
Anonymous

In the inner field: two life trees facing in opposite directions, carrying pomegranate fruits and lotus flowers, terminating in a large lotus. Birds perched on the trees; along the trees, animals (horses) feeding from troughs, on one side; a procession of elephants and one horse, on the other. Broad border filled with leaf pattern.

429 **Kantha**
Jessore, East Pakistan
Embroidered cotton quilt; 2'6¾" x 2'6"
Late 19th century
Asutosh Museum of Indian Art, University of Calcutta #7388

Amidst the usual symbols and figures are Durga on her lion—surrounded by marching soldiers, others are on horseback and elephant.

430 **Kantha**
Jessore, East Pakistan
Embroidered cotton quilt; 2'6" x 2'3½"
Early 20th century
Anonymous

Prominence of central lotus, surrounded by lotus plants, peacocks and "Kalka" border.

428 detail

435 detail

431 Kantha
Jessore, East Pakistan
Embroidered cotton quilt; 1'9¾" x 8¾"
19th century
Asutosh Museum of Indian Art,
University of Calcutta #T.1921

Lotus life tree in central panel.

432 Kantha
Faridpur, East Pakistan
Embroidered cotton quilt; 5'3¾" x 4'2½"
19th century
Published: *Journal of the Indian Society of Oriental Art,* l.c., Plate 10.
Anonymous

The main effect of this rectangular
Kantha is due to the large lotuses, one in
the center, the others along the sides, those
in the corners replacing the "life trees."
Bird, fish, horse and elephant disposed over
the Kantha and on top, Indra on his
elephant. Wave border with circles.

433 Kantha
Colour Plate XLVI
Faridpur, East Pakistan
Embroidered cotton quilt; 2'5½" x 2'6¼"
2nd half 19th century
Anonymous

Lotus life trees springing from quartered
lotuses in the corners. Linear sensitivity and
surface animated by "modelling" stitches
balance one another.

434 Kantha
Faridpur, East Pakistan
Embroidered cotton quilt; 5'1½" x 3'8½"
19th century
Anonymous

Filled with foetus-like shapes with raised
arms, or holding sticks. Europeans in
full dress; a doglike animal rearing on
either side of a life tree.

435 Kantha
Colour Plate XLVII (detail)
Faridpur, East Pakistan
Embroidered cotton quilt; 5'6½" x 3'10¼"
Late 19th century
Anonymous

Peacocks and lotus in corners of central
square, elephant riders, equestrian figures,
bodyguards, tiger, monkeys, a peacock
forming a pleasure boat touching a rearing
serpent. Patterning while modelling in
transparent planes, the stitches are variously
directed. Triple serpent wave pattern
as a border motif.

436 Kantha
Faridpur, East Pakistan
Embroidered cotton quilt; 2'8" x 2'6"
1875
Published: *Marg*, III, 1949, 26
(detail).
Anonymous

Though sometimes inscribed with the name of the person to whom a Kantha was presented, a date is very rarely embroidered. Here, however, it is given a rectangular frame above serpents, life trees, glass lamp and equestrian figure, next to a house boasting many glass lamps in perspective.

437 Kantha
Faridpur, East Pakistan
Embroidered cotton quilt; 3' x 3'½"
2nd half 19th century
Published: *Marg,* III, 1949, 27.

Diagonal stems of life trees organize the excited design. Inserted in branches of life trees are: long-necked human heads, figures consisting of human parts, lingas, tortoises, birds, fish, peacocks. Large figure of Shiva as a yogi, holding a rosary, a serpent next to him.

438 Kantha
Faridpur, East Pakistan
Embroidered cotton quilt; 2'6" x 2'7¾"
Beginning 20th century
Published: *Marg*, III, 1949, 28.
Anonymous

Scenes from the life of Krishna in marginal panels between central lotus and life trees in corners; most of the Gopinis wear semi-Western costume. Whirls frame the central lotus also on life trees; earrings in central square; a spatial situation is attempted showing Radha and Krishna enshrined.

439 Kantha
Colour Plate xxxviii (detail)
Faridpur, East Pakistan
Embroidered cotton quilt; 2'5" x 2'5½"
2nd half 19th century
Published: *JISOA,* l.c., Plate 16.2.
Anonymous

In this most colourful, densely embroidered Kantha, one of the four life trees in the corner is replaced by a phantasy of whirls, wheels, and foliage forming three bowers around flamboyantly distorted human figures.

440 Kantha
Faridpur, East Pakistan
Embroidered cotton quilt; 4'8" x 3'5"
End 19th century
Anonymous

The inner field divided in three panels, one rectangle on each side of the central lotus in its square; the one with a large Navanari-Kunjara, an elephant composed of female figures, i.e. of Shakti or power, carrying Indra; next to this the parable of a horse riding a man; the goddess Durga, Shiva as ascetic, fish, birds, mongoose, etc.; on the other side, the corresponding rectangle shows Kama, the god of love, riding a horse composed of female figures; peacocks, monkey, tiger, etc.

In the broad border: The legend of Kamala-Kamini, and the merchant Chand Sadagar in a boat; Shiva riding on Nandi; a European with his Indian girlfriend being rowed in a boat; fish, tortoise, peacocks, etc., and life tree; on the opposite side of the border, a satire on scenes of contemporary life. A man with his wife, carrying his daughter (?) on his shoulder and leading his mother-in-law on a leash; a peacock, a music and dance party under a canopy lit by chandeliers, a life tree; other scenes show a man in the company of a woman and being beaten with a broom by his wife or co-wife who pulls him by his long hair.

441 Kantha
Faridpur, East Pakistan
Embroidered cotton quilt; 2'10¼" x 2'10¼"
2nd half 19th century
Anonymous

Exclusively filled with animal figures in rectangular compartments around central lotus. Fish and lotus borders.

442 Kantha
Plate xli (detail)
Faridpur, East Pakistan
Embroidered cotton quilt; 4'11" x 3'3"
19th century
Anonymous

Animals and symbols patterned by the organization of their stitches fill the main field of the Kantha around a central lotus with op art effect.

443 Kantha
Colour Plate xliii (detail),
Plate xlv (detail)
Faridpur, East Pakistan
Embroidered cotton quilt; 2'5¾" x 2'2"
Late 19th to early 20th century
Anonymous

Scenes from the life of Krishna: a circus party, temple car; the heads of the demon king Ravana on left, "Kalka" life trees in the corners, animals, symbols such as peacock, butterfly.

Omission of body or limbs of figurines; ideational perspective turns the horses to either side of the temple car. This ancient formula can also be seen in a carving from the Swat Valley representing the chariot of the sun-god. (John M. Rosenfield, *The Dynastic Arts of the Kushans,* Berkeley, 1967, Fig. 88, and similarly, although not as bold in the combination of front and profile view, in Sanchi; J. Marshall and A. Foucher, *The Monuments of Sanchi,* Vol. II, Plate 40.)

452 detail

444 Kantha
Faridpur, East Pakistan
Embroidered cotton quilt; 2'9" x 2'9"
Later part 19th century
Anonymous

Candelabra-like stylization of corner
life trees, issuing above quartered lotus
blooms; horsemen above serpents,
and satirical scenes.

445 Kantha
Faridpur, East Pakistan
Embroidered cotton quilt; 1'7" x 1'8"
Late 19th to early 20th century
Published: *Journal of the Indian Society of
Oriental Art,* l.c., Plate 16.
Anonymous

Images, animal and vegetation symbols
are distributed over this Kantha which has
neither border nor central lotus. Kali dancing
on prostrate Shiva; a charnel ground is
suggested by severed limbs, a prowling cat.
Next to the demon's severed head, held
by Kali, Krishna plays the flute, standing on
a lotus overlapping that of Radha who is
being fanned by an attendant. Below,
a serpent, two heraldic peacocks sharing a
serpent, a tree with roots, a bee and
large leaves in the corners.

Inscribed with name of owner.

D. Assam (nos. 446-451)

446 Pradipdan
Asharikandi, Assam
Terra-cotta; 1'6" x 6½"
20th century
Crafts Museum, New Delhi #M/3/66

This lightholder is a syncretistic shape
of traditional motifs. Top broken.

447 Horseman (Toy)
Goalpara, Assam
Painted pith; 1'¾" x 6" x 3½"
20th century
Asutosh Museum of Indian Art,
University of Calcutta #F.624

448 Peacock (Toy)
Goalpara, Assam
Painted pith; 1'7¼" x 8¼" x 4¾"
20th century
Asutosh Museum of Indian Art,
University of Calcutta #F.96

449 Monster Hugging a Man (Toy)
Assam
Painted pith; 10" x 5½" x 3½"
1966
Philadelphia Museum of Art, Philadelphia
#65-200-2

450 Bird-Man
Assam
Painted pith; 11" x 3½" x 3"
1966
Philadelphia Museum of Art, Philadelphia
#65-200-3

451 Squirrel (Toy)
Assam
Painted pith; 8½" x 7" x 4"
1966
Philadelphia Museum of Art, Philadelphia
#65-200-4

**E. Nagaland and North East Frontier
Agency (nos. 452-470)**

452 Effigy of a Woman
Konyak Tribe, Nagaland
Clay painted; 1'⅛" x 5⅞"
20th century
National Museum, New Delhi #64.911

The form of this effigy recalls those
of carved wooden figures.

Cf. V. Elwin, *The Art of the North-East
Frontier of India,* p. 148.

453 Grave Effigy
Konyak Tribe, Nagaland
Wood sculpture in the round; 3'¼" x 10¼"
20th century
National Museum, New Delhi #64.1461

454 Squatting Figure
Konyak Tribe, Nagaland
Wood sculpture in the round; 8⅛" x 3½"
20th century
National Museum, New Delhi #64.947

Cf. V. Elwin, *op. cit.,* p. 166.

455 Squatting Figure of a Warrior
Konyak Tribe, Nagaland*
Wood sculpture in the round and cloth;
1' x 5½"
20th century
Crafts Museum, New Delhi #M/7/1777
*According to the Crafts Museum.
Cf. V. Elwin, *op. cit.,* p. 152, where a similar
figure is assigned to Tirap (N.E.F.A.).

456 Standing Couple
Plate XXIII
Konyak Tribe, Nagaland
Wood; 11⅞" x 5½" x 4⅞"
20th century
National Museum, New Delhi #64.1326

A common motif also on pillars of the
Morungs (male dormitories).

457 Rider (Toy)
Konyak Tribe, Tuensang, Nagaland
Wood and jute fibre; 9¼" x 2" x 7¼"
20th century
National Museum, New Delhi #64.957

Cf. V. Elwin, *op. cit.,* p. 178.

453

458 Konyak Head-Taker's Tally
Mohung, Nagaland
Painted wood sculpture and hair; 1'5" x 4"
1947
Mildred and W. G. Archer Collection #43

Nude figure with long goat's hair ear tassels reaching to the elbow, standing on a stool, left hand on hip, right hand touching right shoulder. Red touched with black.

Carved by Akai of Mohung, Tuensang subdivision, Nagaland; collected by W. G. Archer from the carver at Wakching, 1947.

The Konyak Nagas live on the northern side, the Phom Nagas on the eastern side of Mokokchung subdivision, Naga hills. Although they speak different languages and comprise separate tribes, Konyak and Phom share a basically similar life. In Naga society, it is necessary that the village young should graduate as warriors. To achieve this status they must either personally take a head or participate in a successful head-taking raid along with others. Further status can be achieved by Feasts of Merit which demonstrate the individual's wealth. For this purpose the mithun (bos frontalis), a great bull, is reared. Its sacrifice involves a great feast in which the whole village shares.

Achievement of head-taker status or the giving of Feasts of Merit entitle a Naga warrior to various privileges publicizing his status. He can: 1. Have carved the front of his house with symbols of his prowess; 2. Wear special tattoo, clothes, and ornaments. The Konyak warrior may wear on his chest a wooden or brass head (no. 461) and a wooden figure tied to his dancing basket. On returning from a successful raid, a dance is held, and warriors wear a pannier-like basket on their hips to which the wooden figure is attached (Note by W. G. Archer).

459 Konyak Head-Taker's Tally
Mohung, Nagaland
Wood; 1'6" x 4"
1947
Mildred and W. G. Archer Collection #44

Nude female figure with flat cap and bangles, hands across belly holding a head. Uncoloured wood with traces of black dye. Eyes made from blue china beads.

Carved by Akai of Mohung, Tuensang subdivision, Nagaland. Collected by W. G. Archer from the carver at Wakching, 1947.

460 Konyak Head-Taker's Tally
Aopao, Nagaland
Dyed wood; 10" x 2¾"
1947
Mildred and W. G. Archer Collection #47

Nude female figure with uncoloured bangles and flat cap.

Carved by Angma, headman of Aopao, Tuensang subdivision, Nagaland, 1947.

461 Konyak Head Pendent for Head-Taker's Necklace
Longkhai, Tuensang subdivision, Nagaland
Wood; 3" x 2½"
1947
Mildred and W. G. Archer Collection #55

Ear broken. Collected by W. G. Archer at Wakching, 1947.

462 Phom Naga Ritual Drinking Mug (Chunga)
Mongnyu (East side) Naga hills, Nagaland
Carved bamboo; 1'4½" x 4"
1945
Mildred and W. G. Archer Collection #24

The carved figures of two small warriors, each standing on a mithun (bos frontalis) head, are holding a chopper (dao) and a head, the other having lost a hand. A deer between the two figures.

Carved by Yakching of Mongnyu, Tuensang subdivision of Nagaland.

The Phom keep ritual drinking mugs in their homes and after their death, these are hung on their graves. The drinking mugs have a triple significance: they are indications of status, tallies of past prowess and auguries for future success. As a result they are carved with figures of the warrior, his victims and the prisoners he has taken.

They also include tigers and king-crows because of their reputation for ferocity. Deer and fishes are portrayed in the hope that the warrior will be as successful in his raids as in his hunting and fishing. Chickens are also introduced because they are sacrificed before going on a raid or during a Feast of Merit. Mithun heads are symbols of well-being since they show the number of Feasts of Merit a man has given. (Note by W. G. Archer.)

All the Chungas with the exception of no. 463 were collected by W. G. Archer from the carvers at Tuensang village, Tuensang subdivision, Nagaland, 1947.

463 Phom Naga Chunga
Carved bamboo; 1'3" x 5"
Ungr, Nagaland
Mildred and W. G. Archer Collection #33

Carved in relief. On one side a warrior holding an upraised Dao and a head in his left hand; small figures on either side; on the other side a warrior with a small figure. Rivers (wavy lines) between the figures.

By Chisidongbang Ao, headman of Ungr, Mokokchung subdivision, Nagaland, 1947.

Chisidongbang Ao told Mr. Archer he was given a sample Chunga by Limnyu (cf. no. 467) from which he made his first carving but he developed a style of his own afterwards. Although Ungr is an Ao Naga village, it borders the Phom Naga country.

462

464 Phom Naga Chunga
Carved bamboo; 1'4½" x 3½"
Mongnyu, Nagaland
Mildred and W. G. Archer Collection #26

The carving shows a nude figure with a
Dao about to attack another figure wearing
a head-taker's necklace. A vertical line
of four heads below a head-taker holding a
Dao and a head, a nude figure beside him.

By Yakching of Mongnyu, Tuensang
subdivision, Nagaland, 1947.

465 Phom Naga Chunga
Mongnyu, Nagaland
Carved bamboo; 1'2¼" x 4½"
Mildred and W. G. Archer Collection #27

With figure of male dancer and a large
mithun the tips of whose horns the hands
of the dancer are grasping. Two king-crows,
one chicken, three fishes.

By Yakching of Mongnyu, 1947.

466 Phom Naga Chunga
Mongnyu, Nagaland
Carved bamboo; 1' x 5½"
Mildred and W. G. Archer Collection #28

Carved with figure of a male warrior
with spear in hand, a cock, two cocks
fighting, a mithun head, a tiger with a split
tail, a Morung (male dormitory) post.

By Yakching of Mongnyu, 1947.

467 Phom Naga Chunga
Mongnyu, Nagaland
Carved bamboo; 1'1½" x 4½"
Mildred and W. G. Archer Collection #31

Carved with large mithun and tiger, two
human heads and a king-crow (drongo).

Carved by Limnyu of Mongnyu, 1947.

468 Mask
Adi Tribe, North East Frontier Agency
Wood; 10¼" x 6⅛"
20th century
National Museum, New Delhi #64.1155

Face green, eyebrows and pupils painted
black, lips red.

469 Dance Mask
Khampti Tribe, North East Frontier Agency
Bamboo and cloth; 1'1½" x 1'4½" x 9½"
20th century
National Museum, New Delhi #64.1320

Facial features painted black on brown cloth..
Eyes painted white and black on affixed
wood (halves of nut shells?). Teeth painted
white on tin. Short russet hair of jute fibres.

470 Mask, Horned
Khampti Tribe, North East Frontier Agency
Cloth, jute fibres and mirrors;
1'1½" x 1'4½" x 9½"
20th century
National Museum, New Delhi #64.1321

Black cloth and blackened jute fibres,
representing a demon in the retinue of Mara,
the evil one, during his attack on
Lord Buddha. Teeth painted white on tin.
Cf. V. Elwin, *op. cit.,* p. 82.

Bibliography

Abbreviations

BDCRI
Bulletin of the Deccan College Research Institute (Poona)

BRMIC
Bulletin of the Ramakrishna Mission Institute of Culture (Calcutta)

BRVRI
Bulletin of the Rama Varma Research Institute (Ernakulam)

EA
Eastern Anthropologist (Lucknow)

FLC
Folklore (Calcutta)

FLL
Folklore (London)

IAEL
Internationales Archiv für Ethnographie (Leiden)

IAL
Indian Art and Letters (London)

IFL
Indian Folklore (Calcutta)

IHQ
Indian Historical Quarterly (Calcutta)

IWI
Illustrated Weekly of India (Bombay)

JAF
Journal of American Folklore (Boston)

JAnthSB
Journal of the Anthropological Society of Bombay (Bombay)

JARS
Journal of the Assam Research Society (Gauhati)

JASB
Journal of the Asiatic Society of Bengal (Calcutta)

JBORS
Journal of the Bihar and Orissa Research Society (Patna)

JGRS
Journal of the Gujarat Research Society (Bombay)

JIAI
Journal of the Indian Anthropological Institute (Calcutta)

JISOA
Journal of the Indian Society of Oriental Art (Calcutta)

Man
Man (London)

ManI
Man in India (Ranchi)

MarchI
March of India (Delhi)

MR
Modern Review (Calcutta)

QJMS
Quarterly Journal of the Mythical Society (Bangalore)

SFQ
Southern Folklore Quarterly (Gainesville, Florida)

WBKL
Wiener Beiträge zur Kulturgeschichte und Linguistik (Vienna)

Abbot, J. *The Keys of Power: A Study of Indian Ritual and Belief.* London: 1932.

Adam, Leonhard. *Primitive Art.* London: 1954.

Archer, Mildred. "Notes on Painting," *Marg,* XX (1966), No. 1, 47.

Archer, W. G. *Bazaar Paintings of Calcutta.* London: 1953.

———. "Diwali Painting," *ManI,* XXIV (1944), 82-4.

———. *Kalighat Drawings.* Bombay: 1962.

———. "Maithil Painting," *Marg,* III (1949), No. 3, 24-33.

———. *The Vertical Man, a Study in Primitive Sculpture.* London: 1947.

Bagchi, P. C. "Female Folk-rites in Bengal," *ManI,* II (1922), 62-8.

Banerji, A. "Phulkaris, A Folk Art of the Panjab," *Marg,* VIII (June, 1955), No. 3, 59-64.

Bhagvat, D. N. *Tribal Culture of the Central Provinces.* Bombay: 1942.

Bhattacharyya, A. "An Anthropomorphic Serpent-Goddess," *FLC,* I (May-June, 1960), 170-77.

———. "The Cult of the Harvest Deities of Bengal," *IFL* (October-December, 1957), 11-8.

———. "Cult of the Smallpox Goddess of West Bengal," *QJMS,* XLIII (1954), 55-69.

———. "Cult of the Tree-Deities of Bengal," *IFL* (October-December, 1958), 26-46.

———. "The Cult of the Village Gods of West Bengal," *ManI,* XXXV (1955), 19-33.

———. "The Cults of the Deified Dead in Bengal," *IFL* (April-August, 1956), 29-39.

———. "Cure-Deities of Bengal," *FLC,* III (February, 1962), 57-68.

———. "The Dharma Cult of West Bengal," *Census 1951, West Bengal (The Tribes and Castes of West Bengal),* V (1953), 351-60.

———. "Puppet Dance in Bengal," *FLC,* I (September-October, 1960), 268-73.

———. "The Rites of the Serpent-Goddess," *FLC,* I (July-August, 1960), 233-40; II (January-February, 1961), 41-8.

———. "Serpent Designs in Bengali Folk Art," *JIAI,* II (1948), 19-28.

———. "The Tiger Cult and Its Literature in Lower Bengal," *ManI,* XXVII (1947), 152-62.

Bodding, P. O. *Folklore of the Santal Parganas.* London: 1909.

———. "Traditions and Institutions of the Santals," *Oslo Ethnografiske Museum Bulletin,* No. 6, 1942.

Bonnerjea, B. "Note on Geometrical Ritual Designs in India," *Man,* XXXIII (1933), 163-64.

Bose, N. K. "The Hindu Method of Tribal Absorption," *Cultural Anthropology* (Calcutta), 1953.

Bose, P. N. "Three Specimens of Santal Drawing," *ManI,* V (1925), 235-36.

Bose, S. K. "Folk Art of Uttar Pradesh," *MarchI,* III (October, 1951), No. 10, 27-8.

Breeks, James W. *An Account of the Primitive Tribes and Monuments of the Nilgiris.* London: 1873.

Brooke, S. C. "The Labyrinth Pattern in India," *FLL,* LXIV (1953), 463-72.

Bulmer, D. "Demon-Worship in Southern India," *JAF,* VII (1894), 156-57.

Cammiade, L. A. "Man-eaters and Were-tigers," *Man,* XXXI (1931), 217-20.

_____. "Man-tigers, Some South Indian Beliefs," *QJMS,* X (1919-20), 37-40.

_____. "The Traditions of the Santals," *JBORS,* II (1916), 15-29.

Census of India. New Delhi (1961), Vol. V, Pt. VII B, Chandras, A. "Gujarat Fairs and Festivals."

_____. New Delhi (1961), Vol. V, Pt. VII A, "Gujarat, Selected Crafts."

_____. New Delhi (1961), Vol. VII, "Kerala, Selected Crafts."

_____. New Delhi (1961), Vol. XIV, Pt. VI B, Village Survey, Monograph No. 6, "Village Panarwa, Udaipur."

_____. West Bengal (1951), see under Ray, S. K.

Chatterji, T. *Alpona.* Calcutta: 1948.

Chattopadhyaya, K. P. "Art of Tribal Folk," *JARS,* XIII (1959), 34-6.

Chaudhuri, N. "The Sun as a Folk God," *ManI,* XXI (1941), 1-14.

Chauhan, B. R. *A Rajasthan Village.* New Delhi: 1967.

Chinmulgund, P. J. "Paithan Painting," *Times of India Annual* (1962), 67-72.

Coomaraswamy, A. K. *History of Indian and Indonesian Art.* New York: 1966.

_____. *The Indian Craftsman.* London: 1909.

_____. "The Nature of Folklore and Popular Art," *IAL,* XI (1937), 76-84; or *QJMS,* XXVII (1936-37), 1-12.

_____. "Picture Showmen," *IHQ,* V (1929).

_____. *La Sculpture de Barhut.* Paris: 1956.

_____. " 'Spiritual Paternity' and the 'Puppet Complex'," *Psychiatry,* VIII (1945), No. 3, 287-97.

Crooke, C. W. "The Cults of the Mother Goddesses in India," *FLL,* XXX (1919), 282-308.

_____. "The Hill Tribes of the Central Indian Hills," *JIAI,* I (1899), 220-48.

_____. *The Popular Religion and Folklore of Northern India.* 2 vols. London: 1896.

_____. *The Tribes and Castes of the North-Western Provinces and Oudh.* Calcutta: 1896.

Crooke, C. W., and Knox, K. N. "Witchcraft in Northern India," *FLL,* XIV (1903), 407-10.

Das, G. N. "The Funerary Monuments of the Nilgiris," *BDCRI,* XVIII (January, 1957), 140-52.

Das, S. R. "A Note on Votive Clay Figurines Used in a Folk Rite of Bengal," *ManI,* XXXII (1952), 105-21.

_____. "Alpana of the Kumari-Vratas of Bengal," *JISOA,* X (1943), 126-32.

Dasgupta, C. C. "Ancient Indian Terra-cottas," *FLC,* I (March-April, 1960), No. 2, 73-80.

Dasgupta, S. B. *Obscure Religious Cults.* Calcutta: 1946.

Datta (Dutt), G. S. *The Folk Dances of Bengal.* Calcutta: 1954.

Dev, C. "An Outline of the Folk Art of Bengal," *IFL* (July-September, 1959), 196-205.

Dey, B., and Irwin, John. "The Folk Art of Bengal," *Marg,* I (1946-47), No. 4, 45-54.

Dey, Mukul. *Birbhum Terra-cottas.* Bombay: 1959.

Diehl, C. G. *Instrument and Purpose; Studies on the Rites and Rituals in South India.* Lund: 1956.

Dimock, E. C. and Ramanujan, A. K. "The Goddess of Snakes in Medieval Bengali Literature," *History of Religions,* I (1962), 307-21; III (1964), 300-22.

Dube, S. C. *An Indian Village.* London: 1955.

Dumont, L. "Definition structurale d'un dieu populaire Tamoul: Aiyanar Le Maître," *Journal Asiatique,* CCXLVI (1953), 256-70.

Durai, H. G. "Preliminary Note on Geometrical Diagrams (Kolam) from the Madras Presidency," *Man,* XXIX (1929), 77.

Dutt, D. "Folk Art and Toys," *IFL* (September-December, 1956), 78-9.

Dutt, G. S. "The Art of Bengal," *MR* (1931), 519-29.

_____. "The Art of Kantha," *MR* (October, 1939).

_____. "Bengali Terra-cottas," *JISOA,* VI (1938), 169-80.

_____. *Catalogue of Folk Arts.* Calcutta: Indian Society of Oriental Art, 1932.

_____. "The Indigenous Painters of Bengal," *JISOA,* I (1933), 18-33.

_____. "The Living Tradition of Folk Arts in Bengal," *IAL,* N.S. X (1936), 22-34.

_____. "Mask Dances of Mymensingh," *MR* (August, 1939), 217-22.

_____. "Tiger's God in Bengal Art," *MR* (1932), No. 2, 521-29.

_____. "A Wood Carving from a Bengal Village," *JISOA,* V (1937), 29-31.

_____. See also Datta, G. S.

Dutta, A. K. "Allegory in Bengal 'Kantha'," *IFL* (January-March, 1959), 64.

Ehrenfels, O. R. von. "Is Aboriginal Art Original?" *ManI,* XXIX (1949), 103-09.

Eliade, M. *Images et Symboles.* Paris: 1952.

_____. *Myths, Dreams and Mysteries.* London: 1960.

Elmore, W. T. "Dravidian Gods in Modern Hinduism," *University of Nebraska Studies,* 1915.

Elwin, Verrier. *The Art of the North-East Frontier of India.* Shillong: 1959.

_____. *The Baiga.* London: 1939.

_____. "Carved Totems of the Uraons," *IWI* (April 5, 1953).

_____. "Folklore of the Bastar Clan-Gods," *Man,* XLII (1943), 97-104.

_____. "The Hobby Horse," *IWI* (July 5, 1953).

_____. "Musical Instruments of Tribal India," *IWI* (November 27-December 4, 1955).

_____. "Myths and Dreams of the Baigas of Central India," *Man,* XXXVII (1937), 13.

_____. "Santal Woodcarving," *MarchI,* VI (1953), No. 2, 17-9.

_____. "Saora Pictographs," *Marg,* II (1948), No. 3, 35-44.

_____. *The Tribal Art of Middle India,* Oxford: 1957.

Emeneau, M. B. "Ritual Games of the Kotas," *BRVRI,* V (1937), 114-22.

Enthoven, R. E. *The Tribes and Castes of Bombay.* 3 vols. Bombay: 1920-22.

Folk Arts of India (Catalogue). Syracuse: 1967.

Fraser, D. (ed.). *The Many Faces of Primitive Art.* Englewood Cliffs, N.J.: 1966.

Fuchs, S. "Clan-God Myths and Worship among the Nimar Balahis," *Essays in Anthropology Presented to Rai Bahadur Sarat Chandra Roy.* Lucknow: 1942, 194-205.

_____. *The Gond and Bhumia of Eastern Mandla.* New York: 1959.

Fürer-Haimendorf, C. von. "Religious Beliefs and Ritual Practices of the Minyong Abors of Assam, India," *Anthropos,* XLIX (1954), 588-604.

_____. *Naked Nagas.* Calcutta: 1962.

Fürer-Haimendorf, E. von. *An Anthropological Bibliography of South Asia.* 2 vols. Paris: 1958.

Ganguli, K. K. "Chamba Rumal," *JISOA,* XI (1943), 69-74.

_____. "Folk-Art of Bengal," *All Indian Folklore Conference Souvenir* (Calcutta), 1964, 22-6.

_____. "Kantha, The Enchanted Wrap," *IFL,* I (April-June, 1958), 3-10.

_____. "Ritual Figures in the Folk Art of Bengal," *IFL* (April-August, 1956), 82-4.

Ganguly, R. N. "Patas and Patuas of Bengal," *IFL* (April-August, 1956), 60.

126

Gazetteer of the Bombay Presidency. IX, Pt. I, 294-311.

Ghose, A. "Old Bengal Painting," *Rupam* (Calcutta), 1926, 27-8.

Ghose, B. *Primitive Indian Architecture.* Calcutta: 1953.

_____. "Traditional Arts and Crafts," *BRMIC,* VIII (January, 1957), No. 1, 6-13.

Ghosh, D. P. "Folk Art of Orissa," *IFL* (April-August, 1956), 73-7.

_____. "An Illustrated Ramayana Manuscript and Patas from Bengal," *JISOA,* XIII (1945), 130-38.

Ghosh, P. C. "The Vastu Yaga and Its Bearing upon Tree and Serpent Worship in India," *JASB,* XXXIX (1870), Pt. I, 199-232.

Goetz, H. *The Art and Architecture of Bikaner State.* Oxford: 1950.

Goldwater, R. *Primitivism in Modern Art.* New York: 1967.

Gordon, D. H. "Korku Memorial Tablets," *Man,* XXXVI (1936), 17-9.

_____. *The Pre-historic Background of Indian Culture.* Bombay: 1958.

Gordon, D. H. and Alchin, F. R. "Rock Paintings and Engravings in Raichur, Hyderabad," *Man,* LV (1955), 97-9.

Goswami, A. *Indian Terra-cotta Art.* New York: 1959.

Gough, E. K. "Cults of the Dead Among the Nayars," *Traditional India,* ed. M. Singer (Philadelphia), 1959, 240-72.

Griffith, C. L. T. "Some Brahmanic String Figures," *Man,* XIV (1914), 92-7.

Grigson, W. *The Maria Gonds of Bastar.* Oxford: 1938.

Gupta, J. *Pragaitihasika Bharatiya Citrakala.* Delhi: 1967.

Harding, S. "The Ramayana Shadow-Play in India," *Asia,* XXXV (1935), 234-35.

Hendley, T. H. "An Account of the Maiwar Bhils," *JASB,* XLIV (1875), 347-85.

Hermanns, Mathias. *Die Religiös-Magische Weltanschauung der Primitivstämme Indiens.* 2 vols. Wiesbaden: 1964.

Hodson, T. C. *The Primitive Culture of India.* London: 1922.

Iyer, Ananta Krishna, L. K. *Mysore Tribes and Castes.* 4 vols. Mysore: 1928-35.

Jayakar, P. "Some Terra-cotta Figurines from Tribal Gujarat," *Marg,* VII (1953), No. 1, 27-32.

Kirkland, E. C. "Bibliography of South Asian Folklore," *Folklore Institute Monograph Series* (Indiana University, Bloomington) XXI (1966).

Koppers, W. "Bhagwan, the Supreme Deity of the Bhils," *Anthropos,* XXXV-XXXVI (1940-41), 325-65.

_____. "Die Bhil in Zentral Indien," *WBKL,* VII (1948).

_____. "Monuments to the Dead Erected by the Bhils and Their Neighbours," *Annali Lateranensi,* VI (1942), 119-206.

_____. "Pferdeopfer und Pferdekult der Indogermanen," *WBKL,* IV (1936), 297-411.

_____. "Zentralindische Fruchtbarkeitsriten und ihre Beziehung zur Induskultur," *Geographia Helvetica,* Vol. I (1946).

Kramrisch, S. *The Art of India.* London: 1965.

_____. *Dravida and Kerala.* Ascona: 1963.

_____. *The Hindu Temple.* 2 vols. Calcutta: 1946.

_____. "Indian Terra-cottas," *JISOA,* VII (1939), 89-110.

_____. "Kantha," *JISOA,* VII (1939), 141-67.

_____. "Kanthas of Bengal," *Marg,* III (1949), 18-29.

Kurulkar, G. M. "Demons of Hindu Mythology," *JAnthSB,* N.S.I. (1946), No. 1, 81-100.

Layard, J. "Labyrinth Ritual in South India," *FLL,* XLVIII (1937), 115-182; LXIII-LXIV (1952-53), 463-72.

Mago, Pran Nath. "Murals and Mosaics from Villages around Delhi," *Design* (New Delhi, August, 1967), 22-5.

_____. "Wall Paintings by Panjabi Peasants," *Design* (New Delhi, October, 1963), 33-6.

Maity, P. K. *Historical Studies in the Cult of the Goddess Manasa* (Calcutta), 1966.

Majumdar, D. N. "The Bhils of Gujarat," *JGRS,* IV (1942), No. 3, 220-37.

Marriott, McKim. *Village India.* Chicago: 1955.

Marshall, Sir J. H. *Mohenjo-Daro and the Indus Civilisation.* 3 vols. London: 1931.

Marshall, Sir J. H. and Foucher, A. *The Monuments of Sanchi.* 3 vols. Calcutta: 1940.

Mathur, J. C. "Domestic Arts of Mithila," *Marg,* XX (1966), No. 1, 44-6.

Meinhard, H. "The Javanese Wayang and Its Indian Prototype," *Man,* XXXIX (1939), 109-11.

Mishra, Binayak. "Folklore and Pauranic Tradition about the Origin of God Jagannatha," *IHQ,* XIII (1937), 600-09.

Mishra, S. "The Folk Art of Mithila," *FLC,* I (September-October, 1960), No. 5, 319-24.

Mitra, K. "The Bird and Serpent Myth," *QJMS,* XVI (1925-26), 180-200.

Mitra, S. C. "Indian Folk-Beliefs about the Tiger," *JAnthSB,* III (1893), 45-60; (1896), No. 1, 80-9.

_____. "Notes on Popular Religion in Bihar," *QJMS,* XXIV (1933-34), 309-13.

_____. "The Peacock in Asiatic Cult and Superstition," *JAnthSB,* IX (1913), 530-44.

Modi, J. J. "A Few Notes on the Ancient and Modern Folklore about the Peacock," *JAnthSB,* IX (1913), 544-54.

____. "The Owl in Folklore," *JAnthSB*, XX (1924), No. 8, 1014-26.

Mookerjea, S. *Folk Art of India.* New Delhi: 1955.

Mookerjee, A. "Bengal Folk Drawings and Paintings," *MR* (1943), 41-5.

____. *Folk Art of Bengal.* Calcutta: 1946.

____. *Folk Toys of India.* Calcutta: 1956.

____. *Indian Primitive Art.* Calcutta: 1959.

Nag, D. S. "Problems of Aboriginals' Crafts," *All Indian Congress Committee, Economic Review,* V (October 15, 1953), 7-9.

Naik, T. B. *The Bhils.* Delhi: 1956.

____. "Some Folk-Elements in Gujarat Culture," *EA,* I (1947-48), 16-26.

Nanavati, J. M., Vora, M. P., and Dhaky, M. A. *The Embroidery and Beadwork of Kutch and Saurashtra.* Baroda: 1966.

Oppert, G. *The Original Inhabitants of India.* Westminster: 1893.

Pal, M. K. *Catalogue of Folk Art in the Asutosh Museum.* Calcutta: 1962.

____. "An Obscure Folk-Cult of Lower Bengal," *IFL* (January-March, 1958), 11-3.

Patel, A. J. "Folk Terra-cottas of Gujarat," *Journal of M.S. University of Baroda,* XII (1963), 63-70.

Pathy, P. V. "Indian Rod Puppets," *MarchI,* II (January-February, 1950), 46-9.

____. "Puppets on the Screen," *Marg,* IV (1950), No. 4, 45-7.

Pischel, R. *The Home of the Puppet-Play.* London: 1902.

Pyyappan, *Lord Ayyappan,* Bharatiya Vidya Bhavan. Bombay: 1962.

Ramanujan, A. K. "The Clay Mother-in-Law," *SFQ,* XX (June, 1956), 130-35.

Ramaswami, M. "Threshold Design; Makolam," *FLL,* XLIX (1938), 181.

Ray, S. K. "The Artisan Castes of West Bengal and Their Craft," *Census of India (West Bengal), 1951* (Calcutta, 1953), 293-349.

____. "Primitive Statuettes in W. Bengal," *Journal of Arts and Crafts* (Calcutta), II (1939), 1-8.

____. *The Ritual Art of the Bratas.* Calcutta: 1961.

Reeves, Ruth. *Cire Perdue Casting in India.* New Delhi: 1962.

Risley, H. *The Tribes and Castes of Bengal.* 2 vols. Calcutta: 1891.

Rivers, W. H. *The Todas.* London: 1906.

Roy, S. C. "The Divine Myths of the Mundas," *JBORS,* II (1916), 201-14.

____. "Magic and Witchcraft on the Chota-Nagpur Plateau—A Study in the Philosophy of Primitive Life," *Journal of the Royal Anthropological Institute,* XLIV (1914), 324-50.

____. *Oraon Religion and Customs.* Ranchi: 1928.

____. "Orientation of Grave-stones and Houses in Chota-Nagpur," *JBORS,* I (1915), 277-80.

____. *The Oraons of Chota-Nagpur.* Ranchi: 1915.

Roy, S. C. and Roy, R. C. *The Kharias.* Ranchi: 1937.

Roy, S. N. "Pradip or Indian Lamp," *JAnthSB,* XIV (1927-28), No. 1, 121-36.

Ruben, W. *Eisenschmiede und Dämonen in Indien.* Leiden: 1939.

Russell, R. V., and Hira Lal. *Tribes and Castes of the Central Provinces of India,* 4 vols. London: 1916.

Sachchidananda. *Profiles of Tribal Culture in Bihar.* Calcutta: 1965.

Saletore, R. N. *The Wild Tribes in Indian History,* Lahore: 1935.

Samanta, S. N. "Some Wooden Dolls of Boro-Balaram," *IFL* (January-March, 1958), 43-7.

Sarkar, B. K. *The Folk Element in Hindu Culture.* London: 1917.

Sen, D. C. "Behula: a Myth of the Snake-Goddess," *MR* (1907), 26-35.

Sen, G. "Purba Varatiya Adibasi Silpa," *Sundaram* (Calcutta), IV-V, n.d.

Shastri, Dakshinaranjan. "Cult and Images of Pitris," *JISOA,* VII (1939), 32.

Singh, Sarva Daman. *Ancient Indian Warfare with Special Reference to the Vedic Period.* Leiden: 1965.

Sinha, Surajit. "Tribal Cultures of Peninsular India," *Traditional India* ed. M. Singer (Philadelphia, 1959), 298-311.

____. "State Formation and Rajput Myth in Tribal Central India," *ManI,* XLII (1962), 25-80.

Skeat, M. "Snakestones and Stone Thunderbolts as Subjects for Systematic Investigation," *FLL,* XXIII (March, 1912), 45-80.

Smith, M. (ed.), *The Artist in Tribal Society.* London: 1961.

Sondhi, G. D. "Puppet Dance Drama," *MarchI,* VI (September-October, 1953), No. 1, 22-4.

Srinivasarao, N. "The Folk Art of Orissa," *FLC,* I (May-June, 1960), No. 3, 114-47.

Suryavanshi, B. "The Cottage Industries of the Aboriginals," *FLC,* II (March-April, 1961), No. 2, 78-9.

Tagore, A. *L'Alpona, ou Les Decorations rituelles au Bengale.* Paris: 1921.

Thurston, E. *Castes and Tribes of South India.* 7 vols. Madras: 1909.

____. *Omens and Superstitions of Southern India.* London: 1912.

Tod, James, *Annals and Antiquities of Rajasthan,* ed. C. W. Crooke. 3 vols. London: 1908.

Tucci, G. *The Theory and Practice of the Mandala.* London: 1961.

Upreti, N. R. "Folk Art of Kumaon," *Department of Anthropology, Royal Tropical Institute* (Amsterdam, 1957), 7-9.

Varma, G. L. "The Theory of Creation (Santali and Vedic) and Primeval Home," *Spark,* I (April 30-May 7, 1950).

Vidyarthi, L. P. *The Maler.* Calcutta. 1963.

Walton, J. "The Art of the Kothi," *ManI,* XXV (1945), 14-6.

Whitehead, H. *The Village Gods of South India.* London: 1921.

Wingert, P. S. *Primitive Art.* New York: 1965.

Zealey, P. "The Folk Painters of Jaipur," *MarchI,* VIII (April, 1956), No. 6, 28-30.

Ziegenbalg, B. *Ausführliche Beschreibung des Malabarischen Heydentums,* ed. W. Caland. Amsterdam: 1926.

FLORISSANT VALLEY COLLEGE
ST. LOUIS, MO.

INVENTORY 1983

Book Design:
Murphy Levy Wurman, Architects

Printing:
Falcon Press

Type:
Baskerville, set by
Typographic Service Inc., Philadelphia

Paper:
Champion Papers, Kromekote
Brown Company, Linweave Tarotext

Photographs:
Harry Holtzman, cover, inside cover, plates I-VIII
Pran Nath Mago, plate XXVIII

FLORISSANT VALLEY COLLEGE
ST. LOUIS, MO.

Cover
Horses in a village sanctuary of Mariamman;
Polanalur (Namakkal)